# VOLTAIRE ESSAYS
## AND ANOTHER

The terra-cotta statue of **Voltaire** by Houdon, seen from the spectator's left

# VOLTAIRE ESSAYS

### AND ANOTHER

❧❦❧

*Theodore Besterman*

LONDON

OXFORD UNIVERSITY PRESS

NEW YORK   TORONTO

1962

*Oxford University Press, Amen House, London, E.C. 4*

GLASGOW  NEW YORK  TORONTO  MELBOURNE  WELLINGTON
BOMBAY  CALCUTTA  MADRAS  KARACHI  LAHORE  DACCA
CAPE TOWN  SALISBURY  NAIROBI  IBADAN  ACCRA
KUALA LUMPUR  HONG KONG

**PRINTED IN GREAT BRITAIN**

# Preface

I AM not at all sure that it is a good idea to give permanent life within the covers of a book to words written for delivery to a particular audience or on a special occasion. So far I have resisted the temptation, but recently a kindly critic wrote in the *Revue de littérature comparée* (1960), xxxiv. 293: 'M. Besterman, trop absorbé par ses publications pour écrire beaucoup lui-même, prend volontiers la parole en des occasions solennelles; il s'efforce alors d'éviter l'académisme et parle volontiers en ami, voire en frère, toujours vigilant, du grand homme, dont il a choisi d'être en notre siècle, le porte-parole autant que l'éditeur.' These words describe my intentions so exactly that they were irresistible, and here is the result. I have added some short 'unspoken' papers, and one address on a somewhat remotely related subject, 'The Love of Manuscripts'.

The lecture delivered at the Pierpont Morgan Library has not hitherto been published; most of the other papers have already been printed as pamphlets or in the *Studies on Voltaire and the Eighteenth Century* edited by me at the Institut et Musée Voltaire; one has been reprinted from the *Times Literary Supplement*, and one is an extract from my edition of the *Lettres de la marquise Du Châtelet*. Essays 4, 5, and 10 were written in English, the others in French; of these no. 9 has been translated by me, nos. 2, 3, 6, 8, and 11 by Mrs. Barbara Bray. It must be a trying experience to translate a writer's work into his own language, and subject to his criticism: Mrs. Bray has admirably surmounted this additional difficulty, and I am most grateful to her.

The abbreviation Best. followed by a number refers to my edition of *Voltaire's Correspondence*.

Th. B.

*Les Délices*
*Autumn 1961*

# Contents

# List of Plates

*Both the statue and the bust form part of the collections of the Institut et Musée Voltaire, Les Délices, Geneva*

# *Voltaire*[1]

*à Henri Guillemin*

## I

Au milieu du xviiie siècle la monarchie et la noblesse avaient déjà perdu une grande partie de leur pouvoir. Qu'était donc la société française il y a deux siècles? C'était d'abord la masse du peuple, et le peuple, c'était la misère et l'ignorance, dont peu s'échappaient. Au-dessus du peuple, c'étaient, côte à côte, la religion et la justice, et comme l'a dit Victor Hugo avec une passion qui ne défigure la vérité en rien, la religion c'était l'intolérance, et la justice c'était l'injustice. Advint le mouvement de pensée dirigé et incarné par Voltaire. 'C'est sous la poussée de Voltaire principalement que s'est réalisé le monde moderne, en préparation depuis le début du siècle, où l'état, affranchi de l'église et purement laïque, garantit à chaque citoyen les libertés de la personne, de la pensée, de la parole, de la presse, de la conscience et du culte.' Ainsi s'exprime l'érudit C. Constantin dans le *Dictionnaire de théologie catholique*. On objectera immédiatement que toutes ces libertés ont été souvent et gravement enfreintes depuis, et qu'elles le sont toujours et un peu partout. Cela n'est que trop vrai, et pourtant il est indéniable qu'un changement fondamental s'est produit dans la société humaine. En quoi consiste donc le revirement dont on est d'accord de remercier Voltaire? Je crois qu'il pourra s'exprimer avec précision ainsi: jusqu'à un certain moment la liberté

[1] Discours prononcé à l'inauguration de l'Institut et Musée Voltaire, le 2 octobre 1954, sous la présidence de M. Luther Evans, Directeur-général de l'Unesco, M. Jacques de Bourbon-Busset, Directeur des relations culturelles, Ministère des affaires étrangères, Paris, et M. Marius Noul, Conseiller administratif de la ville de Genève.

intellectuelle existait, exceptionnellement, par l'indulgence des pouvoirs publics; depuis, quand elle n'existe pas, c'est par les abus commis par ces mêmes pouvoirs. Ainsi défini, on se rend compte qu'il serait à peine possible d'exagérer la portée du changement qui s'est produit.

Cette transformation, qui a ouvert le chemin de la dignité et de la maturité de l'homme, fut le résultat d'un lent travail à travers de nombreuses générations humaines: les penseurs, les savants, les artistes y ont contribué, chacun à sa façon. Il serait bien peu philosophique de l'attribuer à un seul homme. Et pourtant.... C'est ainsi que la figure de l'univers physique, telle que nous nous la représentons, est le résultat de longs siècles de réflexion et de recherche: mais pour cristalliser ce lent processus arrive enfin au moment propice l'homme attendu, et c'est Einstein. Cet instant, dans la rude bataille de l'homme pour devenir vraiment homme, de l'homme simplement *sapiens* pour devenir *homo philosophicus*, cet instant donc dans l'histoire de l'humanité, c'est Voltaire. Et de même qu'on peut fixer la date historique à laquelle notre conception de l'univers physique fut transformée, quoique le moment philosophique s'étende à travers les siècles, ainsi l'historien osera-t-il peut-être fixer l'instant catalytique de la transformation sociale de l'humanité: celui où Voltaire a recueilli le jeune Calas sous le toit de cette même maison où nous nous trouvons rassemblés aujourd'hui et qui dès maintenant est au grand homme pour toujours.

## II

Qu'était donc ce phénomène formidable nommé Voltaire? C'était l'homme le plus typiquement, le plus complètement français qu'on eût jamais connu, l'homme qui a exprimé en sa propre personne tout ce qu'a de fin et de noble cette civilisation dont les grands siècles comptent parmi les moments suprêmes de l'esprit humain, et cela d'autant plus parce qu'ils ont créé l'atmosphère qui a permis à Voltaire de se manifester. Mais ce Français fut en même temps le génie le plus universel de son siècle. Il le fut par ses longs séjours en Angleterre, aux Pays-Bas, en Allemagne, en Suisse, par ses nombreuses amitiés dans presque tous les pays d'Europe, par les visites de centaines d'étrangers venus lui rendre hommage, par son innombrable correspondance, qui comprend des lettres en anglais, en italien, en allemand, en espagnol, en latin, par ses lectures étendues et profondes; mais il le fut surtout en lui-même, parce qu'il sentait pour tous les hommes, et parlait un langage que tous ont compris.

Celui qui a abattu le temple de la superstition et de l'intolérance fut élevé par les Jésuites, et n'a jamais cessé de témoigner de son affection et de sa gratitude envers ses maîtres. Né au XVIIᵉ siècle à l'apogée de l'ancien régime sous Louis XIV, il a vu vers la fin de sa vie le premier triomphe public de ses principes, puisque les événements du 14 juillet à Paris ne sont venus que compléter ceux du 4 dans le nouveau monde. Celui dont le nom est inscrit dans le testament de Ninon de Lenclos, née quelques années après la mort d'Henri IV, a béni le petit-fils de Benjamin Franklin. Descendant d'une modeste famille de robe, sans profession bourgeoise, n'ayant jamais touché un sou des énormes bénéfices rapportés par les milliers d'éditions dans toutes les langues de ses innombrables écrits, Voltaire est mort un des plus grands, des plus puissants et des plus riches seigneurs de l'Europe. Le sage de Ferney a débuté comme poète de salon, mais à l'âge de 24 ans, il devint, avec *Œdipe*, le maître de la littérature française, et le resta jusqu'à son apothéose et sa mort, 54 ans plus tard — il faut s'exprimer ainsi puisque Voltaire, fécond en tout, l'a été même en matière d'apothéoses: il en eut deux, dont l'une de son vivant.

Mais laissons là les paradoxes de cette existence prodigieuse — il semble impossible d'en parler sans multiplier les superlatifs. Jetons plutôt un coup d'œil rapide sur l'essentiel de Voltaire: son œuvre. Notons seulement en passant que le style de Voltaire, ce style miraculeux de grâce, de souplesse, de justesse, d'énergie, de coulante simplicité, ce style voltairien qui semble être une extension presque palpable de la personnalité de l'ecrivain, et non pas un outil péniblement forgé — ce style nous fournit la preuve la plus éclatante de la justesse du mot de Bernard Shaw, lui-même un styliste incomparable: 'Celui qui n'a rien à affirmer n'a pas de style et ne peut en avoir: celui qui a quelque chose à affirmer ira aussi loin dans la force du style que le permettent l'importance de ses idées et l'intensité de sa conviction.'

### III

Est-il possible, pourtant, de résumer l'œuvre de Voltaire, cette cataracte inépuisable de vers et de prose, de tragédies et de comédies, de poèmes épiques et héroï-comiques, de romans et de contes, de science et d'histoire, de philosophie et de métaphysique, de discours, de rapports diplomatiques et de placets, de dictionnaires, de commentaires, d'articles de journaux, et enfin de lettres, ces 18 000 lettres survivantes qui constituent le triomphe de l'esprit, la gloire de la littérature, la délectation du lecteur, et le désespoir de l'éditeur? Non, cela n'est guère possible, mais n'est-il pas triste que parmi ces dix millions de mots il n'y en ait que quelques milliers qui soient toujours lus? Faut-il conclure que *Candide* (écrit sous ce toit), que cette incarnation du génie est tout ce qui reste de bien vivant dans l'œuvre de Voltaire? Non certes. Il est vrai que dans son théâtre Voltaire même n'a pas pu se défaire des langes d'un faux 'bon goût'; mais n'oublions pas qu'*Œdipe*, *Zaïre*, *Mérope* et bien d'autres pièces ont fait l'extase de leurs contemporains, que pendant presque un siècle Voltaire a partagé à égalité avec Racine et Corneille la scène tragique de la Comédie Française. Il faut, bien sûr, que nous ayons le courage de notre propre goût, mais le goût subit de bien étranges transformations, et dans ce domaine encore moins qu'ailleurs, il n'est pas de jugements absolus.

Il est vrai également que toute l'élégance, tout le charme, tout le ton ravissant des petits poèmes de Voltaire, toute l'éloquence des épîtres, des odes et des contes, n'ont point suffi à tirer la poésie lyrique française de son morne silence de deux siècles. Et quoique les contemporains de Voltaire en eussent été convaincus, ni l'épopée noble de la *Henriade*, ni la plaisante *Pucelle* n'ont doté, et de très loin, la littérature française d'une *Odyssée*, d'une *Enéide*, d'une *Divina Commedia*, ou d'un *Paradise Lost*.

Ce que Voltaire a produit dans chacun de ces genres ferait la fortune de tout autre écrivain; mais pour lui il est bon d'être sévère, et nous en avons les moyens, puisqu'il nous reste tant de richesses! Il y a toute cette extraordinaire série de contes en prose, *Candide* n'étant ni seul, ni du tout hors concours. Il y a cet *Essai sur les mœurs*, la première histoire universelle moderne, dont le vol d'aigle, l'éloquence magnifique forment une véritable anthologie de l'esprit 'humaniste' et de la prose française, et qui mérite d'être présenté d'une manière convenable au lecteur de nos jours. Il y a ce *Siècle de Louis XIV* dans lequel Voltaire a fait le premier la peinture d'une civilisation et d'une époque dans ses pensées et dans ses actions créatrices. Il y a ces *Lettres philosophiques* et ces *Eléments de la philosophie de Newton* dont les brillantes lumières ont chassé (pour toujours? espérons-le) les dernières ténèbres remplies de terreurs médiévales. Il y a tous les morceaux iconoclastiques étincelants de verve, d'humour, de malice, d'érudition, cachés sous des titres alphabétiques. Il y a cette série immense d'essais petits et grands encore plus profondément enterrés par les éditeurs sous le titre rébarbatif de mélanges. Il y a, oui, il y a encore beaucoup de produits de cette fécondité inépuisable, mais insistons un peu sur ces mélanges. Qui de nos jours connaît même le titre des *Colimaçons du révérend père L'Escarbotier*, du *Sermon du papa Nicolas Charisteski prononcé dans l'église de Sainte-Toleranski*, du *Mandement du révérendissime père en dieu Alexis*, de l'*Instruction du gardien des capucins de Raguse*, du *Catéchisme de l'honnête homme*, de l'*Avis important d'un gentilhomme à toute la noblesse du royaume*, et de tant d'autres sages leçons et cris d'indignation? Or, parmi toutes ces pièces alphabétiques et mélangées il n'y en a pas une de banale ou d'ennuyeuse; elles portent bien au contraire sur chaque page l'évidence lumineuse de tout ce qu'on entend par l'esprit de Voltaire: intelligence, pénétration, imagination, compréhension, clairvoyance, sagesse, humour, courage, générosité, compassion, tolérance, énergie, verve, variété, ironie, malice, grâce, finesse, brillant, subtilité, éloquence, savoir, sensibilité, noblesse, charme, vivacité, fécondité, style, lucidité, oui, surtout et toujours, raison, lumière, vérité et clarté.

Prenons deux extraits seulement, choisis presque au hasard à un demi-siècle d'intervalle. Voici quelques lignes de l'essai *A M\*\*\** de 1727:

Lorsque je débarquai auprès de Londres, c'était dans le milieu du printemps; le ciel était sans nuages, comme dans les plus beaux jours du Midi de la France; l'air était refraîchi par un doux vent d'occident, qui augmentait la sérénité de la nature, et disposait les esprits à la joie: tant nous sommes machines, et tant nos âmes dépendent de l'action des corps! Je m'arrêtai près de Greenwich, sur les bords de la Tamise. Cette belle rivière, qui ne se déborde jamais, et dont les rivages sont ornés de verdure toute l'année, était couverte de deux rangs de vaisseaux marchands durant l'espace de six milles; tous avaient déployé leurs voiles pour faire honneur au roi et à la reine, qui se promenaient sur la rivière dans une barque dorée, précédés de bateaux remplis de musique, et suivis de mille petites barques à rame; chacune avait deux rameurs, tous vêtus comme l'étaient autrefois nos pages, avec des trousses et de petits pourpoints ornés d'une grande plaque d'argent sur l'épaule. Il n'y avait pas un de ces mariniers qui n'avertît, par sa physionomie, par son habillement, et par son embonpoint, qu'il était libre, et qu'il vivait dans l'abondance.

Quelle simplicité miraculeuse! et que cette simplicité, qui déguise l'art, renferme de coloris et de nuances!

Ecoutez maintenant le préambule d'un petit manifeste de 1770, la *Requête à tous les magistrats du royaume*:

La portion la plus utile du genre humain, celle qui vous nourrit, crie du sein de la misère à ses protecteurs:

Vous connaissez les vexations qui nous arrachent si souvent le pain que nous préparons pour nos oppresseurs même. La rapacité des préposés à nos malheurs n'est pas ignorée de vous. Vous avez tenté plus d'une fois de soulager le poids qui nous accable, et vous n'entendez de nous que des bénédictions, quoique étouffées par nos sanglots et par nos larmes.

Nous payons les impôts sans murmures, taille, taillon, capitation, double vingtième, ustensiles, droits de toute espèce, impôts sur tout ce qui sert à nos chétifs habillements, et enfin la dîme à nos curés de tout ce que la terre accorde à nos travaux, sans qu'ils entrent en rien dans nos frais. Ainsi, au bout de l'année, tout le fruit de nos peines est anéanti pour nous. Si nous avons un moment de relâche, on nous traîne aux corvées à deux ou trois lieues de nos habitations, nous, nos femmes, nos enfants, nos bêtes de labourage également épuisées et quelquefois mourant pêle-mêle de lassitude sur la route. Encore si on ne nous forçait à cette dure surcharge que dans les temps de désœuvrement! Mais c'est souvent dans le moment où la culture de la terre nous appelle. On fait périr nos moissons pour embellir des grands chemins....

On nous dépouille de nos champs, de nos vignes, de nos prés: on nous force de les changer en chemins de plaisance; on nous arrache à nos charrues pour travailler à notre ruine, et l'unique prix de ce travail est de voir passer sur nos héritages les carrosses de l'exacteur de la province, de l'évêque, de l'abbé, du financier, du grand seigneur, qui foulent aux pieds de leurs chevaux le sol qui servit autrefois à notre nourriture.

Tous ces détails des calamités accumulées sur nous ne sont pas aujourd'hui l'objet de nos plaintes. Tant qu'il nous restera des forces, nous travaillerons: il faut ou mourir, ou prendre ce parti.

C'est aujourd'hui la permission de travailler pour vivre, et pour vous faire vivre, que nous vous demandons.

## IV

Dans une de ses pensées, un de ces fragments de lui-même que Pascal a sacrifiés devant nous, le sombre poète s'écrie: 'Qu'on ne nous reproche donc plus le manque de clarté, puisque nous en faisons profession. Mais que l'on reconnaisse la vérité de la religion dans l'obscurité même de la religion, dans le peu de lumières que nous en avons, et dans l'indifférence que nous avons de la connaître.' A quoi répondit le jeune Voltaire:

'Voilà d'étranges marques de vérité qu'apporte Pascal! quelles autres marques a donc le mensonge? Quoi! il suffirait pour être cru, de dire, je suis obscur, je suis inintelligible!' (*Lettres philosophiques*, XXV. xviii).

Quand Voltaire a écrit ces mots il avait presque toute sa vie d'homme pensant devant lui, mais ils contiennent déjà tout le programme de ce demi-siècle de réflexion et d'action, de fécondité génératrice et régénératrice. Ils comprennent presque tous les mots-clef de l'idée voltairienne. Notre grand homme était en effet pour la lumière, et contre l'obscurité; pour la vérité, et contre le mensonge; pour la lucidité, et contre l'inintelligibilité. Voltaire s'attaquait impitoyablement à la notion, redevenue malheureusement un peu à la mode dans les écrits de philosophie et même d'érudition de nos jours, selon laquelle obscurité est synonyme de profondeur, et simplicité de superficialité. En vérité, pour être clair il faut avoir compris: 'Rien ne marque mieux un esprit juste et droit', a dit Voltaire dans une lettre (19 février 1750), 'que de s'exprimer clairement. Les expressions ne sont confuses que quand les idées le sont.' Pour résumer, s'il fallait inventer pour Voltaire un slogan, le voici tout fait: RAISON ET CLARTÉ.

v

Voltaire s'oppose donc à la révélation, au jugement par le cœur, à l'explication de l'inconnu par l'inconnu. Mais la raison a besoin de faits comme point de départ; or, de vastes catégories de faits nous restent inconnues, donc soustraites au jugement de la raison; là Voltaire ne nie pas, puisque nier sans possibilité d'analyse intellectuelle est aussi peu rationnel que croire dans les mêmes conditions. Donc en métaphysique Voltaire est agnostique, mais il accepte de se plier aux conventions de son temps et il donne le nom de dieu à l'ultime inconnu ('Deo erexit Voltaire'). On se prend compte des réserves de Voltaire dans ce domaine par sa définition hautement scientifique de l'âme: 'un terme vague, indéterminé, qui exprime un principe inconnu d'effets connus' (premiers mots de l'article 'âme' du *Dictionnaire philosophique*).

Voltaire n'est pas non plus moraliste dans le sens philosophique du mot: pour lui il n'y a pas de sens moral inné, la moralité est relative, il n'y a que la justice et la conscience sociale, nées de la raison.

Il est évident que Voltaire ne croyait pas à la religion: il était aussi contre les religions, et surtout contre la catholique romaine. Pour Voltaire la religion, n'étant pas basée sur la raison, n'est que superstition; dans une nation policée, la loi doit être juste et suprême, et la religion par conséquent inutile. Il est donc néfaste d'entretenir une organisation autoritaire, dogmatique et intolérante, créée pour maintenir une superstition devenue inutile: conclusion que Voltaire a consacrée par cette exhortation lucide, lapidaire et à l'époque triomphante, Ecrasez l'infâme!

Tel était le côté négatif, destructif, de la pensée de Voltaire: pour bâtir il faut d'abord déblayer le sol. Toutes les grandes vérités, Bernard Shaw nous l'a dit, commencent par des blasphèmes; et les blasphèmes de Voltaire étaient précieux dans ce sens. Par ce moyen il a démontré que le système qui semblait à ses contemporains une cage de fer n'était en réalité qu'une toile d'araignée. Le côté destructif de l'enseignement de Voltaire était donc nécessaire, voire indispensable; mais à longue échéance c'est le côté positif qui doit retenir notre attention.

Que devrait donc être selon lui une société basée sur la raison et la moralité utilitaire? D'abord qu'elle garantisse la liberté de pensée. Cela est évident, puisque la vérité est le résultat de la réflexion. On lui porte donc atteinte au moment où on limite pour quelque motif que ce soit le libre jeu de l'esprit humain. Là encore Voltaire nous a dotés d'une sentence qui résume et perpétue toute une philosophie: 'La liberté est la santé de l'âme.'

Le principe fondamental de la liberté de pensée détermine tout une série d'autres libertés. Ou plutôt la liberté constitue une chaîne: détruisez un maillon et le tout se disloque. Raisonner est une discipline précieuse pour l'individu, mais la pensée ne devient utile pour la société que lorsqu'elle est communiquée. S'ensuit la nécessité de la liberté d'expression, dans toutes ses modalités.

Mais à quoi bon posséder la liberté de penser et d'exprimer sa pensée si cette dernière, et même la première, nous expose à des sanctions? Ce serait le banquet des Barmécides. Voltaire donc a été amené à souligner l'importance de la liberté de la personne et de la propriété, ce qui pose tout le problème de la réforme légale et pénale. Pourtant l'individu n'est qu'une partie de la collectivité, et cette collectivité est gouvernée. Il faut donc qu'elle le soit de façon à obéir aux règles de conduite déjà acquises. L'homme a besoin d'être libre; la liberté dépend des lois; le meilleur gouvernement est celui dont les lois conservent à chacun, sans distinction, le plus de liberté dont il peut profiter sans nuire aux autres membres de la collectivité.

La philosophie de Voltaire se résume donc ainsi: l'action de l'homme doit être basée sur la raison, complétée par la moralité sociale et la sensibilité esthétique. 'Wisdom excelleth folly as far as light excelleth darkness.'

## VI

A présent nous remarquons une chose curieuse, si curieuse, si étonnante, qu'elle fut unique. Nous avons jeté un coup d'œil, très rapide il est vrai, sur l'être prodigieux que fut Voltaire: mais nous avons tout de même évoqué sa vie et sa personnalité, son œuvre et sa pensée. Or quand on a parlé de la vie, de l'œuvre et de la pensée d'un homme de lettres, que reste-t-il? Pourtant nous n'avons fait qu'une allusion à ce qui est le plus connu de Voltaire, à ce qui a le plus contribué tant à sa renommée qu'à l'efficacité de la révolution intellectuelle qu'il a conduite: je veux parler de son action. Voltaire en effet a été le premier d'une lignée honorable d'hommes d'étude qui se sont jetés dans la mêlée pour le bien de la généralité. Voltaire fut aussi le premier depuis vingt siècles qui ait prêché d'exemple.

C'est ainsi qu'il a toujours soutenu les jeunes et les talents, la liste en est longue, et qu'il est toujours venu au secours de ceux qu'atteignait l'injustice, dont la liste est plus longue encore. C'est ainsi qu'il a stimulé autour de lui la culture des champs et les manufactures, qu'il a bâti et semé. Et tout cela il l'a fait non seulement sans encouragement, mais en dépit d'oppositions fanatiques à un point aujourd'hui inimaginable. Nous avons vu que le pouvoir résidait dans l'église et dans la magistrature. Or Calas, pour ne citer que ce seul cas parmi tous ceux dont Voltaire s'est occupé, a été emprisonné, condamné et torturé à mort par l'église et la magistrature la main dans la main. Voltaire, seul, s'est élevé contre elles, son cri d'indignation s'est répercuté autour du globe, et a finalement triomphé. Les hommes se sont tout à coup aperçus que même les pouvoirs les plus écrasants sont incapables de résister à l'indignation provoquée par l'injustice. Cette leçon, Voltaire l'a donnée le premier et pour toujours; depuis le jour où Voltaire, sous ce toit, a ouvert ses bras à la famille Calas, l'injustice sociale est sur la défensive.

Hélas, cette horreur de l'injustice qui fut l'élément le plus profond du caractère de Voltaire, n'a été pour lui-même qu'une source de malheur. La répulsion qu'il ressentait contre elle faisait si intimement partie de son tempérament qu'il l'éprouvait en toute occasion: l'ingratitude d'un ami, la malice d'un censeur, la carence d'un fonctionnaire, toutes ces petitesses l'exaspéraient et le faisaient souffrir et réagir à un point qui ne cesse d'étonner les esprits moins sensibles. Essayons de comprendre cette grande âme: même un Voltaire ne peut pas toujours se libérer des défauts de ses qualités.

## VII

Je vous ai cité Pascal, que Voltaire admirait comme un génie d'éloquence mais qui représentait pour lui l'ennemi: l'esprit d'école, le dogmatisme, l'intolérance, le pessimisme, l'obscurantisme. Ecoutez encore Pascal:

En voyant l'aveuglement et la misère de l'homme, et ces contrariétés étonnantes qui se découvrent dans sa nature; et regardant tout l'univers muet et l'homme sans lumières, abandonné à lui-même, et comme égaré dans son recoin de l'univers, sans savoir qui l'y a mis, ce qu'il y est venu faire, ce qu'il y deviendra en mourant, j'entre en effroi comme un homme qu'on aurait porté endormi dans une île déserte et effroyable, et qui s'éveillerait sans avoir aucun moyen d'en sortir: et sur cela j'admire comment on n'entre pas en désespoir d'un si misérable état.

L'accord d'orgue est magnifique, mais il est faux. Voltaire a donné sa réponse dans les *Lettres philosophiques* (XXV. vi); elle est anéantissante; mais je préfère terminer en vous citant une autre réponse qu'il a faite, en passant, et qui résume toute sa pensée (*A une dame ou soi-disant telle*):

> Je lis au cœur de l'homme et souvent j'en rougis.
> J'examine avec soin les informes écrits,
> Les monuments épars et le style énergique
> De ce fameux Pascal, ce dévot satirique,
> Je vois ce rare esprit trop prompt à s'enflammer.
>     Je combats ses rigueurs extrêmes:
> Il enseigne aux humains à se haïr eux-mêmes,
> Je voudrais malgré lui leur apprendre à s'aimer.

# Voltaire Judged by Flaubert[1]

*to Jean Dutourd*

## I

EVERYONE knows how Flaubert worked: first the slow development at the unconscious level of everyday life; then the sudden precipitation of an idea through the occurrence of some catalytic event, some image seen by chance, some unexpected meeting, or a few words overheard in the street. Then the formulation of a plan, then of another, then of a whole series of plans. Then research, reading, note-taking; and finally, after a year, or five, or ten, the real work begins: he starts to write. It is at this point that the creative process of Flaubert diverges from that of Voltaire. With Voltaire too an important work derived from a mixture of inspiration, reflection, and sheer labour; but when he finally sat down at his desk, Voltaire wrote as a bird sings, clearly, lucidly, with a natural, flowing beauty ('clair comme du Voltaire', Flaubert used to say).[2]

When once the work was finished, Voltaire used to correct much and often, but it was almost always later, as a result of new thoughts or new observations. What a contrast to Flaubert, who wrote painfully, recast every sentence twenty times, and would spend whole days poring over one page! Voltaire wore the French language like a suit made to measure. For Flaubert it was steel armour to which he had to adapt himself with patience, enormous effort, resolution, even violence. That is the difference between genius and talent, even the

---

[1] A lecture delivered to the Société d'histoire et d'archéologie of Geneva, 13 November 1952.

[2] June 1852, ii. 434; i.e. in a letter of June 1852, to be found on p. 434, vol. ii, of the Conard edition.

greatest. Voltaire forged his instrument once for all. Flaubert had to remake his every time.

So it is not surprising that we have a large number of works by Voltaire and few drafts and notebooks, whereas with Flaubert there are quantities of notes but few publications.

A large proportion of the documents that Flaubert accumulated has been preserved for us by the piety of his niece. They now constitute one of the treasures of the library of Rouen where no doubt they will become the delight of scholars. There is another series of notebooks in the historic library of the city of Paris, where as chance would have it they are on the same shelves that hold the Voltaire manuscripts. Chance also has it that among the Flaubert manuscripts which have escaped these collections there is a set of notes, and that these notes consist of the comments and extracts that the novelist made when reading Voltaire's *Essai sur les mœurs*. This precious document has up to the present been preserved from the avidity of collectors, and I have had the happiness of acquiring it for the Institut et Musée Voltaire.

These notes and quotations, written very small on fourteen large pages, present a certain number of difficulties. Neither the writing nor the layout makes for legibility. It is not always easy to distinguish between Flaubert's own comments and his quotations from Voltaire, for his use of quotation marks is capricious, and he often makes a transition in the middle of a sentence. Fortunately Flaubert has indicated the edition he used: he wrote '1784' at the top of the first page. The first attempt at verification showed that he used the Kehl edition, and simply made a small slip. He should have put 1785. Thereafter Flaubert refers to volumes, then chapters or pages, and he always quotes with unusual exactness, reproducing Voltaire's text letter for letter; his scruples extend even to indications of omissions. The great documentary novelist is at work—even if the references are not always quite precise.

The examination of this manuscript made a pleasing respite in the midst of far more arduous studies. Not that this little notebook of Flaubert's contains anything sensational. But everything Flaubert wrote is precious, and when it concerns Voltaire it acquires a special importance, not only because Voltaire is Voltaire, but because he was the writer who most influenced Flaubert, as we shall see. And let us not forget that the *Essai sur les mœurs* is one of those masterpieces of our culture which are nowadays neglected, and Voltaire's most important achievement.

## II

Flaubert plunges directly into Chapter XVII, 'manners, government, and customs about the time of Charlemagne'. He thus skips all the preliminaries of Voltaire's great work of synthesis—400 pages on ancient history, mythology, the history of the Jews, the history of the East, &c. In Chapter XVII, he says,

there bursts forth in an almost lyrical manner the sorrow Voltaire felt when he thought of the centuries of barbarism that followed the splendour of the Roman Empire. 'What was there to prevent these new-comers from putting up regular buildings on the Roman model? They had the stone, and the marble, and finer woods than we have. ... Why were all those comforts unknown that sweeten the bitterness of life, if not because the savages who crossed the Rhine made the peoples they found there as savage as themselves?'[1]

Flaubert then singled out for comment a rather odd series of subjects: the origin of confession, the origin of the Waldensians, the Trojan horse, the tale of a king of Lorraine and his wife, whom he accused of committing incest with her brother, William the Conqueror, Henry IV, Emperor of Germany, the greatness of the Holy See, the strange ceremonies at the coronation of the popes, the feudal system, armour, the coinage, the chastity of Louis VIII, King of France, the Crusades, Saladin,

[1] f. 1r.; K. [xvi]. 409; M. xi. 268. The references are to Flaubert's manuscript, the Kehl edition, and the Moland edition. The quotation marks missing from the text have been restored; the references left incomplete by Flaubert have been completed.

the capture of Constantinople, Voltaire's use of antithesis, the story of the six burghers of Calais who offered their lives, the plague of 1348, the question whether Henry V was King of France, the Maid, language, Pope Pius II, the anecdote about Tamburlaine and a Persian poet, the allegation that Louis XI poisoned his brother, the social organization and climate of Switzerland, the orders of chivalry, the Wars of the Roses, Ximenes, Galileo, the battle of Pavia, Thomas More, the religions of England, the Jesuits, the Daughters of Charity, the Inquisition, albinos, the Battle of Lepanto, the issue of blood, the massacre of St. Bartholomew, Philip II, the conversion of Henri IV, the story of the false Dimitri, Shah Abbas, the expulsion of the Moors, the martyrs, laws, a story about the emperor of China and an historian.

It would be pointless to look for any other unifying principle in this wonderful catalogue than that Flaubert made it. One could make an equally interesting and equally varied list of the subjects that Voltaire treated but Flaubert left out. The novelist noted and commented on different parts of Voltaire's great work for various reasons: sometimes to agree, sometimes to satirize; here he finds a fine phrase, there he finds one to make fun of; first it is the writer, the student of prose, who speaks, then it is the neurotic expressing his disgust with life.

'When once a language begins to take shape, it is an instrument which great artists find ready to hand and which they make use of without bothering their heads over who governs or otherwise troubles the earth'[1]—small wonder that this sentence attracted Flaubert's attention, for it expresses the whole philosophy of that knight of the ivory tower; and he adds, 'His artistic independence, a rare thing in one who apparently took little account of the absolute or of pure beauty, bursts forth in this sentence with a kind of secret joy'.[2]

In the same way Flaubert noted certain passages that showed the injustice of the criticisms levelled against Voltaire. He quotes:

[1] f. 3v; K. [xvii]. 376; M. xii. 61.          [2] f. 3v.

The soul of Hadrian IV was all the nobler because his origins were lowly. The Roman church has always had the advantage of being able to accord to merit those things which are elsewhere accorded to birth; it can even be said that the popes who have acted most arrogantly are those who were born in the meanest condition. Today there are some monasteries in Germany that will only receive nobles into their community. The soul of Rom[e] has more greatness and less vanity.[1]

And he comments: 'However unjust some people may make him out to be, Voltaire recognizes the greatness of the Holy See, and the power it derives from election.' Certainly, but Flaubert has been led into error here through not perceiving a characteristically subtle stroke of irony: the German phenomenon to which Voltaire refers was not unknown in France also, as the historian, and his readers, were aware.

On the subject of Joan of Arc, Flaubert notes: 'Where have I read—in M. Villemain perhaps—that Voltaire was guilty of treason against the national honour in his masterpiece? Well, here is what he says about Joan's executioners: "They burned to death the woman who, as the saviour of her king, would have had altars raised in her name in the heroic days when men still honoured their liberators." '[2] But here Flaubert is just being perverse. *La Pucelle* Voltaire's masterpiece? Certainly it is his 'purest' piece of writing in Flaubert's sense of the word, a work with no justification outside itself. But really it takes a Flaubert to consider this poem the masterpiece of the author who wrote the *Dictionnaire philosophique*, the *Siècle de Louis XIV*, *Candide*, not to mention the *Essai sur les mœurs* itself.

'Wherever bloodshed occurs', Flaubert points out, 'or there is murder or carnage, Voltaire always hates it, and takes care to show that he does so. E.g. the Amboise conspiracy: "Those who were caught died under torture, and for a whole month there was nothing to be seen in Amboise but scaffolds and gibbets laden with corpses." '[3] And Flaubert adds a remark

[1] f. 2r.; K. [xvii]. 51 [*sic*, read 53]; M. xi. 402.
[2] f. 3v.; K. [xvii. 358]; M. xii. 49.
[3] f. 5v.; K. [xviii]. 491; M. xii. 500.

which it must be admitted is more worthy of Bouvard and Pécu-
chet than of their creator: 'This is an exaggeration; there were
other things to be seen.'

There are also whole series of phrases that Flaubert picked
out, often, it is true, because he agreed with them, but principally because he admired their lapidary clarity. On the subject
of Saladin and the earthquake of 1182: 'The Turks were told
by their priests that God was punishing the Christians; the
Christians were told that God was punishing the Turks; and
the fighting continued amidst the ruins of Syria.'[1] About the
deputation from Berne to Charles the Bold: 'These citizens of
Berne did not fall on their knees: they spoke with humility and
defended themselves with courage.'[2]

Often Flaubert gives the reasons for his admiration. For
example: 'Here', he says, 'is Voltaire's true style, spirit and
manner, when he speaks of William the Conqueror, who sent
the pope King Harold's standard and part of his treasure in
exchange for the banner the pope had given him.' And he
quotes: 'Thus a barbarian, the son of a prostitute, the murderer
of a rightful king, shares this king's remains with another
barbarian; for take away the names of Duke of Normandy, of
King of England, and of pope, and the whole thing becomes
nothing more than the exploit of a Norman thief and a Lom-
bard receiver: and that in fact is what all usurpation boils down
to.'[3]

In Flaubert's opinion 'Voltaire's frequent antitheses are
right, because they come naturally and as if imposed by the
inevitability of the fact'.[4] Elsewhere he exclaims: 'Fine com-
parisons, fine phrases, fine style', and quotes: 'When we manage
at last to live under tolerable laws, along comes a war to
confuse all boundaries and ruin everything; and we have to
start all over again like ants whose ant-hill has been trampled

---

[1] f. 2*v*.; K. [xvii. 132]; M. xi. 454.
[2] f. 4*r*.; K. [xvii. 474-]475; M. xii. 125.
[3] f. 1*v*.; K. [xvi]. 564; M. xi. 358.
[4] f. 3*r*.

on';[1] and 'thus everything has its contradiction, and we drift about in a vessel for ever tossed by contrary winds'.[2] It is a little surprising that Flaubert should have chosen these two sentences. They were already fairly hackneyed in the eighteenth century, and hardly seem to deserve the novelist's encomium.

It also happens that Flaubert disapproves of the style of the *Essai*. Thus he quotes: 'All the amenities of society and that sound philosophy without which society has no lasting charm have penetrated into those parts of Switzerland where the climate is more pleasant and where abundance reigns. In short in these regions once so rustic they have managed in certain places to unite the politeness of Athens with the simplicity of Sparta',[3] and he adds, 'This only makes us laugh. It is no longer part of our poetic diction.'

Voltaire says that the Inquisition drove Protestants farther away from the Roman Church, 'and the sulphur-reeking gowns of the Holy Office are the standard against which they are united for ever'.[4] 'If he had found this phrase in Corneille', says Flaubert, 'Voltaire would have underlined it and said, "Imagine gowns being a standard!"' True, but Flaubert is being a little hard on his master, of whose critical approach to Corneille, as we shall see, he disapproved strongly, and with justice.

### III

When Flaubert spoke of Voltaire he knew what he was talking about. He had been reading him since the age of fourteen.[5] He analysed scene by scene, in more than 400 pages,[6] all Voltaire's plays, although to tell the truth he found it a tedious business,

---

[1] f. 7v.; K. [xix]. 409 [*sic*, read 410]; M. xxiv. 574; this last reference is not a mistake. The quotation is taken from one of Voltaire's comments on his *Essai*. The modern editors have separated these remarks from the work to which they refer, and placed them among the miscellaneous works. There are innumerable oddities of this kind in the standard editions of Voltaire.

[2] f. 7v.; K. [xix]. 409 [*sic*, read 410]; M. xxiv. 574.

[3] f. 4r.; K. xvii. 475; M. xii. 126.

[4] f. 5; K. [xviii. 264]; M. xii. 353.          [5] 14 August 1835; i. 21.

[6] See the catalogue of the sale of 18–19 November 1931, no. 153; also nos. 112 and 152; and nos. 60–61 of the sales at Antibes, 28–30 April 1931.

and even quoted it as evidence of the robustness of his constitution.[1] Voltaire's stories, he said, 'have an exquisite savour for me. I have read *Candide* twenty times: I translated it into English, and I have read it again since from time to time.'[2] And towards the end of his life, when he was ill and sad, he 're-read for the thousandth time the *Contes* of M. de Voltaire'.[3] Flaubert compared Voltaire faced by his critics to the giant affronting the Lilliputians.[4] After reading a work on Mme Du Châtelet he exclaimed, 'What an intelligent man! And what a good one!'[5]

René Dumesnil, in his admirable *Gustave Flaubert*,[6] an authoritative work, tells us that 'up to the last day of his life Flaubert was to re-read Shakespeare and Goethe, Byron and Hugo; always, with the same youthful ardour, giving expression to his wonderment. But in the same way he was to read Racine and Voltaire, Montaigne and Boileau.' Now these words give a very misleading impression. They set Voltaire, together with Racine, Montaigne, and Boileau, below Shakespeare, Goethe, and Byron in Flaubert's mind. This is very sweeping, and as far as Voltaire is concerned, simply untrue. It is not my present intention to prove what I say by recalling Voltaire's influence on the novelist's work. That would take far more time than I have at my disposal. Some other time. But at least it is an indisputable fact that Flaubert mentions Voltaire's name more often than that of any other writer—leaving out of account, of course, Hugo, Maupassant, and other contemporaries.

(I have just mentioned Montaigne, and cannot resist interpolating a strange remark of Flaubert's: 'Montaigne's mind', he said, 'is a square, Voltaire's is a triangle.' Even if one doesn't quite understand, one feels he is saying something very true.)

[1] August 1845, 8–9 May 1852, 2 July 1853; i. 189, ii. 409, iii. 260.

[2] 7 June 1854; iv. 154: cf. 6–7 June 1853; iii. 288.

[3] 19 October 1875; *Correspondance: Supplément*, edd. René Dumesnil, Jean Pommier, and Claude Digeon (Paris 1954), [iii]. 223.

[4] 20 October 1835; i. 59.

[5] 27–28 August 1846; i. 275.     [6] 3rd edition (Paris 1947), p. 309.

I don't mean to say that Flaubert was a blind disciple of his great predecessor. He profoundly admired his prose,[1] but he also found it 'dry as tinder'.[2] Voltaire's style 'dry as tinder'! But we mustn't be too severe. Flaubert was often ill, and even Homer nods.

But Flaubert was capable of worse things when he rode his artistic hobby-horse at random. One day he wrote to Louise Colet:

> People go into ecstasies over Voltaire's correspondence. But *that* was all the great man was ever capable of—that's to say, of *expounding his personal opinion*; all his work is that. That's why he is so pitiful as a dramatist, and in pure poetry. He wrote one novel, the epitome of all his work, and the best chapter of *Candide* is the visit to Signor Pococurante, where again Voltaire expresses his personal opinion about practically everything. These four pages are one of the marvels of prose writing. They contain the essence of sixty volumes of writing and half a century of effort. But I defy Voltaire to describe a single one of those pictures by Raphael that he mocks at. What seems to me to be the highest thing in Art (and the most difficult) is not to make people laugh or cry, nor to fill them with desire or rage, but to do what nature does—that is, *make people dream*.[3]

At the same time Flaubert showed a remarkable critical insight into Voltaire. No one but Flaubert ever thought of applying the term 'spicy' to Voltaire—and yet how true and appropriate it is! When he says, 'but for Racine, Voltaire would have been a great poet',[4] and that Voltaire was 'cramped by Boileau',[5] he voices an insufficiently recognized truth. For in fact the life of Voltaire the artist is a tragedy, the tragedy of a man of genius bound hand and foot by a 'good taste' that was alien to him, indeed hostile to his proper powers. One is struck by the fact that Voltaire's strictly literary works show little artistic development: *Irène* is not superior to *Œdipe*, nor

[1] 7 June 1844; i. 154.       [2] 6–7 June 1853; iii. 231.
[3] 26 August 1853; iii. 322.       [4] 8–9 May 1852; ii. 409.
[5] 14 October 1846; i. 377.

*Le Taureau blanc* to *Zadig*, nor *La Guerre civile de Genève* to
*Le Temple du Goût.* This fact is the more strange and instructive because it relates to the man whose intellectual evolution
took him from the college of Saint-Louis to Ferney, that is to
say from the Middle Ages into the future. Flaubert didn't find
*that* truth in his school-books.

He exclaims elsewhere apropos of Corneille, 'What a vile
piece of work are M. de Voltaire's commentaries!'[1] If I dared
to interpret what Flaubert was thinking, I should say that
what he found so objectionable was the fact that Voltaire
commented on the plays of Corneille with reference to no
other standards than the rules accepted by Corneille himself.
No progress is possible by such a method. Indeed, this part of
Voltaire's criticism is no more than superficial, and only now
and again do we see the luminous clarity of which he was so
eminently capable.

On the philosophical plane, too, Flaubert said some pro-
found things, such as these words, worthy of Voltaire himself:
'They're going to send soldiers and guns against the Moslems.
What they ought to send is a Voltaire.'[2] At the end of 1867, at
a time when only the most clear-sighted were beginning to have
an inkling of what was in store for France, Flaubert was saying:
'If we'd continued along the high road of M. de Voltaire,
instead of being led astray by Jean-Jacques into neo-Catho-
licism, barbarism, and fraternity, we shouldn't be where we
are now.'[3] And again, 'If we have sunk so low morally and
politically, it's because instead of following the high road of
M. de Voltaire, i.e. of Justice and Law, we have taken the by-
ways of Rousseau, which have led us, via "feeling", back to
Catholicism. If we had worried about Equity instead of Fraternity, we should have been all right.'[4] To appreciate these words
at their true worth one needs to understand Flaubert's ter-
minology. In particular, one needs to know what he means by

---

[1] 15–16 May 1852; ii. 413; cf. 7 September 1853; iii. 336.
[2] 4 September 1858; iv. 278.          [3] 15 December 1867; v. 344.
[4] End of December 1867; v. 348–9.

'fraternity'. But even without understanding every nuance or sharing all Flaubert's opinions, one can recognize what he says as the words of a man who read history with rare understanding, and who saw clearly what Voltaire stood for, indeed still stands for, in the intellectual development of our troubled centuries.

I end with a final quotation, which represents Flaubert's considered judgement, so to speak, on Voltaire. 'I regard M. de Voltaire', he wrote to Mme Roger Des Genettes about 1859–60,[1]

as a *saint*! Why do people persist in trying to see a humorist in a man who was really a fanatic? M. de Maistre said of him in his treatise on *Sacrifices*: 'There is no flower in the garden of the mind that this caterpillar has not defiled.' I can no more forgive M. de Maistre for this phrase than I can forgive Messieurs Stendhal, Veuillot, and Proudhon for their judgements. They're all the same: cranky and anti-art. Temperament counts for a good deal in our literary tastes. Now, both were great men, but I love Voltaire as heartily as I detest Rousseau, and the difference between your taste and mine troubles me. I'm astonished you don't admire that great heart-beat that stirred the world. Could anyone achieve such results without being sincere? In your opinion on this you belong to that school of thought in the eighteenth century itself, which saw nothing in religious enthusiasm but the play-acting of priests. Let us bow down before all altars! In short, Voltaire seems to me to have been a man of magnificent passion, determination, and conviction. His 'Ecrasons l'infâme!' ('Let us crush the infamous') is for me like the summons to a crusade. His whole intelligence was an instrument of war. And what endears him to me still more is the contempt I feel for the so-called Voltairians, who laugh at all the things that are important! Did Voltaire laugh? No—he gnashed his teeth!

[1] iv. 363–4.

# Voltaire and the Lisbon Earthquake
## or, The Death of Optimism[1]

*to René Varin*

### I

AT dawn on Saturday, 1 November 1755, there was a slight haze over Lisbon, one of those mists that promise a sunny morning. By half-past nine the mist had already dispersed. It was fine and mild. The sun was shining. There was no wind. The sea was calm. An unusual silence hung over the city: it

[1] A public lecture delivered at the University of Geneva on 10 November 1955, to mark the bicentenary of the earthquake at Lisbon. For the scientific details of the disaster the author consulted Francisco Luiz Pereira de Sousa, *O terremoto do 1º de novembro de 1755 em Portugal* (Lisbon 1919–32), the third volume of which is devoted to Lisbon. For contemporary accounts, see principally the articles in the *Journal encyclopédique* and the 'Mémoires de Trévoux'; pamphlets of which a certain number are listed by B. Rohrer, *Das Erdbeben von Lissabon in der französischen Literatur des achtzehnten Jahrhunderts* (Heidelberg 1933); and G. Gastinel's article 'Le Désastre de Lisbonne', *Revue du dix-huitième siècle* (Paris 1913), i. 396–409; (1914), ii. 72–92. For the history of earthquakes, the works of Montessus de Ballore and Perrey, and Frédéric Montandon's very useful summary, *Les Tremblements de terre destructeurs en Europe* (Geneva 1953), have been consulted; for the theory of earthquakes in general, Charles Davison, *A Manual of Seismology* (Cambridge 1921); for the history of philosophical optimism, Otto Lempp, *Das Problem der Theodizee in der Philosophie und Literatur des 18. Jahrhunderts* (Leipzig 1910), Paul Hazard, *La Pensée européenne au XVIIIᵉ siècle* (Paris, 1946), ii. 49–70, and W. H. Barber, *Leibniz in France from Arnauld to Voltaire* (Oxford 1955); see also W. Lütgert, *Die Erschütterung des Optimismus durch das Erdbeben von Lissabon 1755* (Beiträge zur Förderung christlicher Theologie, v. iii: Gütersloh 1901). Sir Thomas Kendrick, who had in the press a substantial study on the Lisbon disaster, since published, was kind enough to read the manuscript of the present lecture, and give the author the benefit of his valuable advice. An interesting catalogue has been published under the title *Exposição iconográfica e bibliográfica comemorativa da reconstrução da cidade depois do terremoto de 1755* (Lisbon 1955).

was the feast of All Saints, and those who were not already in church were getting ready to go there. For Lisbon was a devout city, one of the chief centres of the Holy Office, especially distinguished by the great number of its churches, monasteries, relics, and miracle-working statues, by the extreme luxury of its religious rites, and by the violence of its piety at all levels of society.

At this hour many of the faithful were still in the streets, glancing up at the calm sky as they went along, for suddenly a long rumbling was heard, like the sound that heralds a storm in the distance. But the people did not have time to be astonished: the rumbling was not coming from the sky, but on the contrary from the bowels of the earth, and it was followed by a violent shock, and another, then a third, then a whole series. The ground buckled up and split open. Buildings already shaken crashed into the rifts, and men, beasts, and carriages were engulfed. The disturbance of the earth was prolonged under the sea, and as a result the upheaval in the city was accompanied and followed by huge tidal waves as tall as houses. But even they were not enough to quench the fires that had by now broken out all over the capital. A few hours later the centre of Lisbon and a large part of the districts built on neighbouring hills were no more than blazing ruins, the faithful crushed to death in their churches, the Inquisition and the prisoners of the Inquisition in their dungeons, the rich in their palaces, the poor everywhere. Bits of houses floated about in the harbour, fragments of ships lay in what had been the public squares. The streets were covered with mud and ashes. Ten thousand corpses lay under the ruins or scattered about on the ground. No one knew how many had been injured. All who could still walk had fled. Only a few monks and priests stayed to protect the churches' buried treasures, and to implore, too late, God's mercy. When the sun went down the silence of despair and death reigned over the city, broken only by the groans of the wounded, men and horses, the howling of dogs, and the roar of the hungry flames.

The earthquake extended across the whole of the Iberian peninsula and the seas surrounding it. Setubal and other small towns were destroyed. At Cadiz eighteen tidal waves, one after the other, drowned 200 people, among them Racine's grandson. All Europe and parts of North Africa felt the aftermath of the shock. The surfaces of various lakes were disturbed as far away as Scotland and Sweden, and shocks were registered even in the Azores and New England. On 9 December the shock reached the Haut-Valais: Brigue and other places were either entirely destroyed or badly damaged. On the 10th Voltaire wrote to Tronchin, the banker, that Lake Léman 'was suddenly completely covered by a thick cloud, though the sun had just been shining brightly. It was twenty minutes past two, and we were sitting at table in our little Délices—it didn't disturb our dinner.' On the 26th it was the turn of the region that includes Aix-la-Chapelle, Liège, and Maestricht. On 20 February 1756 the Duchess of Saxe-Gotha wrote to Voltaire from Gotha, 'we experienced last Wednesday a slight earth-tremor which caused us to quake a little, privately, here in the castle, and made the citizens of the town tremble outright'. Two days later Sébastien Dupont wrote to Voltaire from Colmar: 'There has been an earthquake here. The wind did terrible damage. The din lulled one philosopher to sleep; but it kept plenty of other people awake.'

In Lisbon itself intermittent shocks continued for ten years.

II

But all this was of comparatively minor importance. In fact the moral repercussions of this event exceeded by far its physical and even its personal consequences. Two centuries afterwards the mere name of Lisbon has a tragic sound even for those who know nothing about the disaster. This is not really surprising, for when it happened the earthquake of 1 November 1755 fell like a thunderbolt on the whole of the Western world, and wrought a permanent transformation in every thinking man's philosophy.

Of course no generalization as sweeping as that can be absolutely true: but I think that by and large it is true enough. For example, it is often maintained that the great men of the Victorian age—of whom Gladstone is the archetype—were sturdy optimists. They were nothing of the kind. The idea is even an instructive example of the lack of clarity and the semantic confusions that are unfortunately so characteristic of our own times. The so-called optimists of the last two centuries were in fact meliorists. But to believe in perfectibility is not the same thing as to believe that all is for the best in the best of all possible worlds. It is the exact opposite. This was not recognized 200 years ago, but a hundred years after that the fact could no longer be doubted. It is quite possible, therefore, to be an 'optimist' in the popular sense of the word, and at the same time to be the exact opposite according to its real meaning.

If, then, the Lisbon disaster overthrew one of mankind's most intimately cherished beliefs, how did this transformation come about? Was it the unusualness of the event, or was it the intrinsic nature of it, that caused such a reaction? Was it because men's minds were ready for the change, and only awaited some external stimulus to turn the intellectual balance? Was it a consequence of the development of the means of communication, which enabled the news to travel round quickly? All these explanations carry a certain amount of weight. But are they enough?

### III

Science has made such rapid progress in our time that we tend to think of our fathers' knowledge as elementary, and flatter ourselves that our grandfathers lived in an intellectual world entirely different from our own. Nothing could be farther from the truth. In the eighteenth century cultivated people were already forming a reasonably just idea of the earth's very modest position in relation to the rest of the universe. They thought of our 'insignificant globule' as a fragile structure,

composed of unstable elements held together by a relatively
thin crust of which the components vary from place to place.
They knew it revolved round the sun at a dizzy pace, and that
it also revolved on its own axis. They were apprehensive about
the countless dangers to which the earth is exposed, the fragments of matter that hurtle through space, the rain, hail, and
snow, the raging winds, thunder and lightning, hurricanes and
water-spouts. They already had vague ideas about the layer-
like structure of the earth, and of the dangers arising from the
constant disturbances that seemed to afflict the mysterious
depths of the globe.

In theory, then, earthquakes were nothing surprising for
an educated man of the eighteenth century, and in practice
everyone was quite used to them. Earth-tremors were commonplace, not to say frequent, incidents: even for those periods
and regions known at that time, that is, before systematic
records began to be kept, we have more or less accurate
records of thousands of earth-tremors. A fair number of these
surpassed the Lisbon earthquake in violence: to go no farther
back, there were those that occurred in Basle in 1356, in Lower
Austria in 1590, and in Ragusa in 1667. Quite a number
exceeded the Lisbon disaster even in the extent of the damage
they did and the number of victims they claimed: those, for
example, in Villach in 1348, in the Abruzzi in 1456, in Bene-
vento in 1688, and in the central Apennines in 1703. And this
does not include volcanic eruptions, tornadoes, floods, epi-
demics, and the even more dreadful disasters that man con-
trived for himself. People ought to have been quite hardened
to the idea of cataclysms. And so they were. And what is more,
the medieval terror of phenomena that were 'against nature'
had been dispelled by the prediction of Halley's comet, which
had lent great force to the mechanistic explanation of the
universe.

So if the Lisbon disaster had such a shattering effect, it was
certainly not, in the main, because of its mystery, its unusualness, or its extent.

## IV

Were men of intellect specially impressionable by such occurrences as the Lisbon earthquake? On the contrary. Man's confidence in himself and his own destiny was at its highest peak. Optimism was both a function and a necessary condition of progress. The idea that man is always advancing had become almost instinctive. When one is convinced that everything *tends* towards good it is very human, even if not very logical, to conclude that everything *is* good. This notion permeated the Western world almost completely, much encouraged by the doctrines of resignation and submission preached by Christianity. It had also recently received on the one hand its most developed philosophical expression in the *Théodicée*[1] of Leibniz (1710), even if this exposition was unsystematic; and on the other hand its most concise and luminous embodiment in Pope's *Essay on Man*[2] (1733).

Pope abstained from putting a special point of view. On the contrary, as he specifically tells us in his 'Design', his intention was to paint an impartial picture, 'steering between the extremes of doctrines seemingly opposite'. In the following famous lines, with that poetic precision of which he was a master, Pope crystallizes the views then current on the problem of evil:

> Cease then, nor Order imperfection name:
> Our proper bliss depends on what we blame.
> Know thy own point: this kind, this due degree
> Of blindness, weakness, Heaven bestows on thee.
> Submit: in this, or any other sphere,

[1] But the doctrine was implicit in all Leibniz's previous work. Already in 1687 he had said that God 'did everything for the best' (Barber, p. 36); but the word 'optimism' was not invented until later, by the Jesuits of the 'Mémoires de Trévoux' (February 1737), p. 207, in the course of a discussion on Leibniz.

[2] Pope's brilliance cannot disguise his lack of profundity. But at the same time it should be noted that Leibniz's undeniable insight was accompanied by astonishing intellectual lapses. For instance, he ends his discussion of the problem of moral evil with the conclusion that God has allowed it because the world, even with evil in it, is better than any other possible world.

Secure to be as blest as thou canst bear:
Safe in the hand of one disposing Power,
Or in the natal, or the mortal hour.
All Nature is but Art, unknown to thee;
All Chance, Direction, which thou canst not see;
All Discord, Harmony not understood;
All partial Evil, universal Good:
And, spite of Pride, in erring Reason's spite,
One truth is clear, Whatever is, is right.

(*An Essay on Man*, i. 281–94)[1]

This was the point of view of all thinking men, with the exception of certain 'philosophes', who in 1755 had scarcely begun to undermine the enormous self-satisfaction of a world which still thought of itself theologically as being at the centre of a special creation. It was even shared by those who followed the teachings of the church, saving a few shrewd Jesuits who had perceived the dangers it held for Rome.

So the news of the Lisbon disaster did not break upon a public disposed by its beliefs or its intellectual tendencies to be over-impressed.

V

The western invention of printing in the fifteenth century had advanced enormously by the eighteenth. There were still no rapid composing machines or presses capable of turning out thousands of pages an hour, but book-production was now on such a scale that the first bibliography of bibliographies had been published by the seventeenth century. It is estimated that in France in the middle of the eighteenth century at least 2,000 books were printed a year; and Barbosa Machado's *Bibliotheca lusitana*, published 1741–59, necessarily a very incomplete work, lists 25,000 titles of works in Portuguese. Even periodicals were already very numerous. Every large town had its reviews and gazettes, not to mention broadsheets. So a large

[1] The early French translations of this passage are very inaccurate, especially the version by Du Resnel, which was the one Voltaire chiefly consulted when he did not use the English text itself.

number of people now made their living by transmitting news of interesting events to a public immemorially greedy for sensation; and it was not in the journalists' interest to play down the importance of events. Their work was made easier and more effective by the development of postal services and public transport.

This then was another factor that tended to emphasize the importance of a disaster like the one at Lisbon, and to spread the knowledge of it. But it only explains to a limited extent the reactions to the disaster of 1755. Here is the proof of this limited influence. The favourable conditions which I have just outlined were new, it is true, but they dated from more than a few years or even a few decades back. Certainly there was no significant difference between 1755 and 1750. And 1750 had been a sort of *annus mirabilis* as far as earthquakes went. To mention only the most important: on 9 May an earth-tremor had seriously shaken the town of Huelva in Spain; on the 25th of the same month another shock was felt from Bordeaux to as far as Montpellier; on 7 June 2,000 people were killed in an earthquake on the island of Cythera; and lastly on 17 December there was a disastrous tremor of the earth at Fiume, nearly the whole town was destroyed, and an entire island was submerged by the inevitable tidal wave. This rapid succession of major catastrophes was exceptional, and one would have expected the celebrity of Cythera and Fiume alone to attract the attention of news-sheets and their readers almost as much as Lisbon did later on. And yet the journalists of 1750 reacted with no more than slight interest to this accumulation of tragedies, and in the other writings of the time the subject is scarcely mentioned.

What is the explanation, then, of the tremendous impression that was created by the tragedy of 1755?

## VI

A few days after the disaster of 1 November the bankers of Geneva, whose interests were heavily engaged in Portugal as elsewhere, were already receiving news of it from their correspondents. In fact, similar communications are to be found in the archives of many countries. If I single out Geneva it is not from local considerations, but because this was the city that alone presented the phenomenon that was decisive in making the disaster famous—the presence of the man of genius who a few months before had come to live on the outskirts of the city. The bicentenary of this event, of capital importance in the history of ideas, has unfortunately been allowed to pass unnoticed.

On the same day as the tragedy at Lisbon the young Claude Pierre Patu had written from Les Délices to Garrick: 'My dear friend, what a wonderful man is this heavenly songster of the *Henriade*! And what a happiness it is to be able to study such a great mind! Just imagine a man who seems near death, yet has all the fire of his first youth, and the brilliance that we find in his delightful stories!' This great mind, with all its fire and brilliance, with all the wisdom derived from sixty years of reflection, activity, and suffering, was destined to burst soon into fresh flower. The news from Portugal was communicated at once to Voltaire, and on 24 November he wrote to Jean Robert Tronchin, the Genevan banker, at Lyons:

This world is very cruelly organized, my dear sir. They will certainly be hard put to it to puzzle out how the laws of movement can bring about such frightful disasters in *the best of all possible worlds*. A hundred thousand ants, our fellow-creatures, suddenly crushed in our ant-hill, half of them perishing, no doubt, in unspeakable agony beneath wreckage from which they cannot be extricated. Whole families ruined all over Europe, the businesses of a hundred of your countrymen swallowed up in the wreckage of Lisbon. What a sorry gamble is the game of human life! What will the sermonizers have to say, especially if the palace of the Inquisition is still standing? But I trust that at least the reverend father inquisitors have been crushed to death like everyone else. This ought to teach men never to persecute their fellows, for while a few holy scoundrels are burning a few fanatics, the earth swallows them all up indiscriminately!

2. The statue seen from the spectator's right

## VII

For Voltaire, the Lisbon disaster was no more than a last straw. For a long time he had been opposed to Leibniz's ideas and even more to their systematic development by Christian Wolff,[1] and to Pope's epigrammatic simplification. But it was only slowly that he reached his own conclusions. Voltaire was no systematic philosopher: rather, he was a poet who responded with acute sensitivity to the changes and chances in the external world and in his own life. His reactions on the publication of the *Essay on Man* in 1733 show that he was completely unprejudiced. He admires the poem, though he finds it a little obscure (24 July 1733; Best. 614). In the following year (1734), when he wrote the *Traité de métaphysique*, he left aside the problem of evil, considering it a human invention and therefore irrelevant. He concludes: 'It is just as absurd to say of God in this connexion that God is just or unjust as to say that God is blue or square.' In 1735 Pope's *Moral Epistles* in verse were to Voltaire a paraphrase of his own remarks on Pascal in the *Lettres philosophiques* (20 September 1735; Best. 885). But a few months later he wrote to Madame Du Deffand that it was

an odd thing to attribute the irresistible fury with which all kinds of animals destroy each other, to some kind of love of society in God. I agree that there appears to be some sort of design there, but it's a design that certainly can't be called love. The whole of Pope's poem is riddled with this kind of obscurity[2] (18 March 1736; Best. 1002).

Meanwhile, Crown Prince Frederick introduced him to Wolff; Voltaire and the prince began a wide-ranging correspondence on the subject of free-will; the Cirey group studied Leibniz; Mme Du Châtelet finished her *Institutions de physique*, which favoured Leibniz; and Voltaire completed his *Métaphysique de Newton*, which was anti-Leibnizian by implication.

[1] Who wrote *Beweis, daß aus dem Satz: diese Welt ist nicht die beste, lauter absurda fließen.*

[2] This did not prevent Voltaire from classing Pope with Addison, Machiavelli, Leibniz, and Fontenelle among 'many-sided geniuses' (Best. 946).

This intellectual activity reached a temporary culmination in 1744, with Voltaire's reply to a critic: 'Just show me... why so many men slit each other's throats in the best of all possible worlds, and I shall be greatly obliged to you' (March 1744; Best. 2745).

There follow the stories, the first *Memnon* (which later became *Zadig*), *Le Monde comme il va*, the second *Memnon*— all full of sorrow at the spectacle of a world that suffers, but in which Voltaire still hesitates to bring out finally the incompatibility of evil with an optimist teleology. The end of the forties draws near, with the absurd death of Voltaire's brilliant and beloved Emilie, the break-up of the peaceful retreat at Cirey, the Prussian court, Frederick's orange-peel and dirty linen (to adopt the two friends' own description), the unspeakable Frankfurt incident, the pirate booksellers who stole and mutilated his manuscripts, and many other pains and persecutions. And then at last the haven of Les Délices, and Voltaire breathes a deep sigh of relief:

> O Maison d'Aristippe! ô jardins d'Epicure! ...
> Recevez votre possesseur!
> Qu'il soit, ainsi que vous, solitaire et tranquille!

> (Oh house of Aristippus, gardens of Epicurus! ...
> Receive your new possessor!
> May he, like you, know solitude and peace!)

Alas, even this eloquent hymn to liberty and friendship brought trouble, because of too open an allusion to a Savoyard pope of the fifteenth century. The persecutions suddenly began again, and immediately afterwards came the disaster at Lisbon. In the intellectual and emotional situation in which Voltaire then was, its effect upon him was decisive.

### VIII

In fact, from that moment the disaster and all it stood for was to haunt his imagination for ever. His *Poème sur le désastre de*

*Lisbonne* was conceived at once, and must have been written straight off, since it was finished before the end of November.

Voltaire invites those who claim that 'all is for the best' to look on Lisbon, ruined indiscriminately. (It was this same indiscrimination that troubled the young Goethe.)[1] The city

> eut-elle plus de vices
> Que Londres, que Paris, plongés dans les délices?
> Lisbonne est abîmée, et l'on danse à Paris.

> (Was Lisbon then more vile
> Than London, Paris, where men still can smile?
> For Lisbon's swallowed up, and Paris dances.)

'Misguided philosophers' tranquilly seek the causes of the event; they would do better to weep. Is it pride, then, to pity human suffering? How can anyone answer that everything is necessary and good?

> Quoi! l'univers entier, sans ce gouffre infernal,
> Sans engloutir Lisbonne, eût-il été plus mal?
> Etes-vous assuré que la cause éternelle
> Qui fait tout, qui sait tout, qui créa tout pour elle,
> Ne pouvait vous jeter dans ces tristes climats
> Sans former des volcans allumés sous nos pas?
> Borneriez-vous ainsi la suprême puissance?
> Lui défendriez-vous d'exercer sa clémence?

> (Without this horror, would the universe,
> For lack of Lisbon lost, have been the worse?
> Are you so sure that the eternal cause
> That does all, knows all, freely forms its laws,
> Has not the power to make existence sweet
> Without these fiery gulfs beneath our feet?
> The highest pow'r would you have thus confin'd,
> Forbidden to show mercy to mankind?)

No, answers Voltaire,

> Je respecte mon dieu, mais j'aime l'univers.

[1] *Dichtung und Wahrheit*, I. i.

(I honour God, but love the universe.)

Would philosophers have the victims of Lisbon believe that others will benefit from their misfortunes? No—

Dieu tient en main la chaîne, et n'est point enchaîné.

(God holds the cord, but God cannot be bound.)

But why, if he who rules us is just, do we suffer?

Voilà le nœud fatal qu'il fallait délier.
Guérirez-vous vos maux en osant les nier?

(Here is the knot that has to be untied.
But evils can't be cur'd by being denied.)

Voltaire goes on to insist on the existence of evil, and examines it at every angle without reaching a solution.

Leibnitz ne m'apprend point par quels nœuds invisibles,
Dans le mieux ordonné des univers possibles,
Un désordre éternel, un chaos de malheurs,
Mêle à nos vains plaisirs de réelles douleurs,
Ni pourquoi l'innocent, ainsi que le coupable,
Subit également ce mal inévitable.

(If then of all the worlds this is the measure,
How comes it that for every empty pleasure
Some secret process works us lasting pain,
In endless chaos? Leibniz does not explain,
Nor why this same resistless woe should strike
The guilty and the innocent alike.)

A single gleam pierces the darkness:

*Un jour tout sera bien*, voilà notre espérance,[1]
*Tout est bien aujourd'hui*, voilà l'illusion.

(One day all will be well—that is our hope,
All is well now—that is the illusion.)

[1] Voltaire later added a question mark here; see G. R. Havens, 'Voltaire's pessimistic revision of the conclusion of his *Poème sur le désastre de Lisbonne*', *Modern Language Notes* (Baltimore December 1929), xliv. 492.

Pope, piling up epigrams, failed to notice that optimism necessarily entails fatalism, a doctrine hardly less flattering to the Supreme Being than to man. Voltaire was not such a good poet as Pope, but he reasoned better: he understood the implications of the philosophy he was attacking. But that is not the main distinction of his *Poème*, nor the one which renders it unique, or contributed the most towards its remarkable effect. The first works written about the Lisbon disaster, that is to say those few that were composed without knowledge of Voltaire's poem, take in a whole range of sentiment, from total acceptance to anger; only Voltaire, though his work was so rapidly set down, manifests a response that derives basically from a simple, humane impulse of pity. His poem found a response in both the mind and the heart of his generation, and awakened its latent magnanimity.

In short, men were stirred not so much by the disaster itself as by the event seen through the sensibility of a great man. Once again a poet was the legislator of mankind.

IX

Hardly was the *Poème sur le désastre de Lisbonne* finished than it was put into the hands of Cramer, the publisher: it was Voltaire's intention to issue it as a pamphlet, like his epistle in honour of Les Délices. But as always his friends made him waver, and it was not until the early months of 1756 that the poem appeared, accompanied by *La Loi naturelle*. Meanwhile Voltaire had carefully corrected his poem; on 22 March, in an unpublished letter, he told the bookseller Michel Lambert that he had already thrown four proofs on the fire, one after the other. A good while before this, in January 1756 and even in December 1755, the first versions of the *Poème sur le désastre* were known through manuscript copies in all the salons and literary societies of Paris. At that time, this was in fact the normal procedure for all literary works that were unlikely to receive official permission. Even a work as long as *La Pucelle*, and of such a special nature, was known also in 1755 in literally hundreds of manuscripts. They had become valuable international merchandise.

It was thus that Thieriot, an old friend of Voltaire's but one who by no means approved of all his actions, was able to congratulate him on his 'fine sermon on Lisbon'. 'I read it yesterday', he wrote, 'at M. d'Argental's. You've never done anything in this line that's so sustained, so well knit, and so noble, touching, and well written. The thought is as wise as it is free!' He advises Voltaire to be discreet, however, and keep his 'incomparable work' to himself. But it was too late.

The stir caused by the Lisbon poem was enormous: a score of editions in the course of 1756. All the reviews and gazettes began to publish comments on it, and more or less authentic accounts of the disaster. Pamphlets poured out (I have seen a hundred or so just for the years 1756 and 1757); theological, philosophical, and scientific volumes followed, including that of the young Immanuel Kant.[1] Reading this mountain of paper, a Herculean task, one sees from the references, and even quotations, that if this particular event struck so many imaginations it was because Voltaire had provided the impetus. Some of these writings are, of course, only conventional reactions: the orthodox cry blasphemy, the followers of Leibniz hoist the master's standard. The majority of these authors, however, share, and share increasingly, Voltaire's agnosticism and doubt. Among his non-sectarian critics it is impossible to find one that opposes him with any real argument. Even Rousseau's letter of August 1756 is more an emotional reaction than a discussion of a philosophical proposition. Thus he holds men responsible for their own misfortunes because in the case under discussion the earthquake would not have killed

---

[1] *Geschichte und Naturbeschreibung der merkwürdigsten Vorfälle des Erdbebens welches an dem Ende des 1755sten Jahres einen großen Theil der Erde erschüttert hat* (Königsberg 1756). The earthquake even provided a subject for the theatre; see, for example, the letter from Joseph Berchoux to Cavatini about their opera, *Le Désastre de Lisbonne*: Berchoux, *Voltaire, ou le triomphe de la philosophie moderne* (Paris &c. 1814), pp. 217–23.

so many people if they had not been gathered together in a big city.[1] The great dreamer's idea provides an elegant subject for controversy, but it does not get us noticeably nearer the truth. It leaves out of account such catastrophes as hurricanes, which can devastate whole countries; and worse still, it evades the great problem of free-will, of which optimism is only one aspect.

X

As for Voltaire himself, the years that followed Lisbon only increased his pessimism.[2] Already in 1755 he wrote, 'Men do themselves more harm on their little mole-hill than nature does. More men are slaughtered in the wars of our own creation than are swallowed up by earthquakes' (letter to François Louis Allamand, 16 December 1755). The horrors of the Seven Years War, including the execution of Admiral Byng, aggravated this state of mind. Epithets fly one after another in Voltaire's correspondence for the years 1756–8: the world is 'mad', 'completely mad', there is 'nothing madder or more atrocious'. And each time he expresses his disgust there is a sad or sarcastic allusion to 'all for the best', to optimism, to 'the best of all possible worlds' which 'is certainly ugly enough'; 'the earth is steeped in evil, moral and physical'; 'happy the man who can look with a tranquil eye on all the great events in this best of all possible worlds'.

In short, at this period Voltaire had become a man obsessed, tormented by the spectacle of a humanity that suffered and was resigned to suffering. But if he was obsessed, he was also a genius, a creator: it was unavoidable that this preoccupation should work upon every level of his consciousness, develop,

[1] This is by no means to say that Rousseau was not alive to the tragedy of the event. See the eyewitness account both of the disaster and of Jean-Jacques's reaction in [Achille Guillaume] La Bègue de Presle, *Relation ou notice des derniers jours de mons. Jean-Jacques Rousseau* (London 1778), p. 35; I owe this reference to M. Gagnebin.

[2] The word was not invented until 1794, by Coleridge.

form, crystallize, take on an independent life, and be born in the shape of a work of art. And so it was, in *Candide*. The *Poème sur le désastre de Lisbonne* opened the proceedings against optimism; *Candide* closed them with a sentence of death.[1] The Lisbon poem had stirred thinking men and prepared the ground, the furious laughter of *Candide* converted them once for all. Voltaire had always looked on metaphysics with a doubtful eye, but had gone in for it himself. It was a poor sort of science, he admitted, but respectable. Now it had become 'metaphysico-theologico-cosmolonigology'. Voltaire had abandoned argument for irony. But he left no room for the smallest doubt of his conviction that belief in optimism was a mere straw that humanity clung to so as not to drown in the tempest of misfortunes.

But it is the end of *Candide* which represents the real intellectual revolution of its day: the *Poème sur le désastre de Lisbonne* concluded on a note of hope; later, as we have seen, Voltaire added a question-mark. It may have been at this time that he re-read Pope, and, coming on his exhortation to hope, exclaimed in the margin: 'What can I hope when all is right?'[2] In *Candide* this is all set on one side as irrelevant, and for theories, speculations, and abstractions Voltaire substitutes, through the voice of Candide, a concrete saying: 'We must cultivate our garden.' Voltaire had realized that the doctrine of optimism was in reality the opposite of what it seemed: philosophical optimism is really a doctrine of despair, an anti-social belief, 'A cruel philosophy under a consoling name' (letter to Elie Bertrand, 18 February 1756). If all is for the best in the best of all possible worlds, what is the use of bothering? Just let events lead us where they will, and let us abandon ourselves to fatalism. No, replies Voltaire, all is not for the best

[1] Paul Hazard (ii. 67) writes that with *Candide* 'the case is over and the cause is lost'; Barber (p. x) says the same thing in different words when he states that the year 1760 'marks the end of the period in which Leibnizian metaphysics and Leibnizian optimism were matters of topical importance'.

[2] George R. Havens, 'Voltaire's marginal comments upon Pope's *Essay on Man*', *Modern Language Notes* (Baltimore November 1928), xliii. 435.

in this world; what is good does not make up for what is bad; good will not increase nor will evil diminish, just on their own, through the operation of laws invented by metaphysicians. On the contrary, it is up to us to haul ourselves out of the Slough of Despond. We must act. We must cultivate our garden.[1]

Bolingbroke, who was a friend of Voltaire's even before the young philosopher's visit to England, who was also a friend of Pope and was soon to suggest his *Essay on Man*, had written in 1724 to Voltaire (Best. 185): 'If you succeed in rooting out the tares [from your heart], the good seed will grow abundantly.'[2] Was not this the life Voltaire led after *Candide*? When he saw evil he tried to destroy it; he encouraged the good seed to take root wherever it could.

It was in this way, through the catalytic effect of the Lisbon disaster, that Voltaire became the sage of Les Délices and Ferney, the active conscience of an age, the prophet of reason and of the offspring of reason—understanding, tolerance, and peace. That was how Voltaire cultivated his garden.

[1] The different interpretations of the end of *Candide* are examined by William F. Bottiglia, 'Candide's garden', *Publications of the Modern Language Association of America* (Menasha, Wis., September 1951), lxvi. 718–33. By a pure chance that is nevertheless striking, the last speech delivered by the sturdiest 'optimist' of the old school, Gladstone, was addressed to a rural society. He ended by exhorting its members to cultivate their garden.

[2] For all that concerns the related subjects of Bolingbroke, reform, and the symbol of the garden, see the significant phrase in the letter to Alembert in December 1757, only a few months before *Candide* was written: 'It only needs four or five philosophers to get together to overturn the Colossus. It's not a question of stopping our servants from going to mass; it's a question of depriving heads of families of the tyranny they've usurped, and of inspiring a spirit of tolerance. This great mission has already had encouraging successes. The vine of truth has been admirably cultivated by men like d'Alembert, and Diderot, and Bolingbroke and Hume. . . .'

# Voltaire's commentary on Frederick's
# L'Art de la guerre

## I. THE MANUSCRIPT

THE king's poem *L'Art de la guerre* was probably written about the middle of 1749, under the inspiration of a meeting with Maurice de Saxe. This passage from a letter to Voltaire of 15 July 1749 may be compared: 'J'ai vu ici [Berlin] le héros de la France [Maurice de Saxe].... Je me suis instruit par ses discours, non pas dans la langue française, mais dans l'art de la guerre.' On the other hand, we find the king asking his ambassador in Paris, Le Chambrier, on 19 December 1750, that is, after the marshal's death, to procure him a copy of the latter's manuscript 'Visions militaires' (*Politische Correspondenz Friedrich's des großen*, viii. 197), which were not published until 1757. And on 8 April 1751 Frederick tells his brother Henry: 'J'ai reçu les *Rêveries* du comte de Saxe, qui m'ont fait grand plaisir, et, pour le surpasser en folie, je me suis avisé de mettre en vers les préceptes de cet art...' (op. cit. viii. 322). The implication is as untrue as it is pointless (or at least it seems so, but then Frederick always had a motive for the least of his actions), for the *Art* was privately printed in 1749[1] and was submitted to Voltaire for annotation by the spring of 1751 at the latest, as we shall see when the *Correspondence* reaches that year. The fifth book was in his hands when he went to the Marquisat in March (letter to Darget of the 11th).

Voltaire had Frederick's text transcribed by Collini on the

---

[1] This can be inferred from references in Frederick's correspondence with Darget in May 1749: the poem in 28 'feuilles' there mentioned can only be the *Art de la guerre*; see the *Œuvres de Frédéric* (ed. Preuss; quarto edition), xx. 27–30; it should be noted that by 'feuilles' Darget means 'leaves', not 'sheets'.

right-hand pages of folded leaves, the facing ones being left blank for Voltaire's notes. The resulting manuscript of 92 leaves (172 written pages) came into the possession of the Gräfin von Itzenplitz-Friedland,[1] later entered the Königliches, afterwards renamed the Brandenburg-preußisches, Hausarchiv at Charlottenburg, and is now in the Deutsches Zentralarchiv at Merseburg, by the courtesy of whose director I was allowed to have it microfilmed.

Frederick rewrote the *Art* with Voltaire's commentary before him; this work was completed in July/August 1751 (see Koser-Droysen, ii. 346), and the resulting version became the authorized text, which was first published in the 1752 edition of the *Œuvres du philosophe de Sans-Souci*,[2] whence it passed into all the subsequent editions. This is hereafter referred to as the published, revised, or authorized version.

Voltaire refers from Frederick's text for the most part by means of letters of the alphabet, which have been retained as he wrote them. It should be borne in mind that in doing so he did not always refer to that particular word only: sometimes he is pointing to the phrase or even to the whole line of which it forms part. The text of his note immediately makes this clear. Voltaire also made a certain number of emendations on the right-hand pages, that is, directly on the text. A further complication is created by the fact that Frederick, although he made the bulk of the changes on his own copy of the poem, also made a certain number on the right-hand pages of the manuscript before us.

The translation of the manuscript into print was therefore rather difficult.[3]

---

[1] *Œuvres de Frédéric*, vol. x, p. iv.

[2] But in my copy (now in the Institut et Musée Voltaire) of the very rare 1750 edition the text of the *Art* (at the end of vol. ii) is the revised one: this merely proves that this text (which has separate pagination) was inserted into some copies of the 1750 edition to replace the original version.

[3] A fragment of Voltaire's notes, on the beginning of book i, was published as long ago as 1849 in the *Œuvres de Frédéric*, x. 334–49, where they have remained unnoticed ever since: they have not been included among Voltaire's

References to Voltaire's commentary are given thus: i. 2. c, that is, book i, f. 2, note c.

## II. THE POEM

*L'Art de la guerre* is in six books and about 1,600 lines, being second in length among the king's voluminous verse compositions only to the *Palladion. Longo intervallo,* the *Art de la guerre* and the *Palladion* hold the same places in Frederick's literary output as do the *Henriade* and the *Pucelle* in Voltaire's. This is probably no chance coincidence: Frederick flattered his master even to that extent.

Voltaire calls the *Art de la guerre* a didactic poem: he might equally well have termed it autodidactic, for, though its poetic structure is confused, the *Art* appears to be addressed to Frederick himself. The opening lines:

> Vous qui tiendrez un jour par le droit de naissance
> Le sceptre de nos rois...

make this clear. It is true that as he advances Frederick gets more and more confused, addressing now a soldier, now an officer, now a commander. However, Frederick undoubtedly wrote the poem partly as a literary exercise, partly to fix the principles of war in his own mind. Of course these considerations did not exhaust the king's motives: for politics and propaganda were never out of his mind.

It is not necessary to evaluate the poem in any detail as literature: it is confused in structure, feeble in execution, commonplace in poetic style; the kind of examination to which Voltaire subjects it could easily be multiplied two or three times in extent. It is true that in reading the version published in Frederick's works one is struck by not infrequent felicities of imagery and style: these are nearly always in Voltaire's lines,

works, nor recorded by Bengesco, nor mentioned in works on Voltaire's and Frederick's poetics. Apart from this small fragment the commentary had not been previously printed until it appeared in *Voltaire Studies* with the present explanatory text.

or in those modelled on or even direct echoes of passages in Boileau or in Voltaire's writings, chiefly the *Henriade*.

The most interesting feature of the poem itself is the light it throws on Frederick's character and opinions.[1] It must be remembered that this is a didactic poem, and that it is written, as it were, in the first person: its views are Frederick's views; the poem need not, indeed must not, be treated as a work of the imagination. A detailed analysis would take us too far afield, but one point is obvious on the most casual reading: the king was obsessed by the need for the minute planning and the most cautious execution of every undertaking. This characteristic was manifested in all Frederick's actions, not excluding his relations with Voltaire. I have already had occasion to refer to this more than once in notes on the *Correspondence*.

### III. THE COMMENTARY

The outstanding thing about Voltaire's notes on the *Art de la guerre* is not the fact that they yield over 300 new lines of his verse: for after all they are discontinuous fragments, and rewritings of another man's work at that. Still, so many new lines from Voltaire's pen cannot but be of interest.

More important, however, is the recovery of so extensive a demonstration, with examples, of Voltaire's poetic principles. Of course his writings, not least his correspondence, are filled with systematic and passing comments in this field, but in the way of specific commentary we have only that on Corneille (M. xxxi–xxxii), the brief and restrained notes on two epistles by Helvétius (M. xxiii. 6–23), and the forgotten notes on Frederick's *Ode aux Prussiens* (*Œuvres de Frédéric*, x. 322–30). In the present text, and this is the feature of outstanding importance, we have sustained criticism illustrated by numerous examples composed *ad hoc*. We have a text, Voltaire's

---

[1] It is surprising therefore that no study has ever been made of *L'Art de la guerre*; it is not so much as mentioned by Gertrud Jagdhuhn, 'Die Dichtungen Friedrichs des Großen', *Romanische Forschungen* (Erlangen 1936), l. 137–240.

comments on it, and over 300 lines as rewritten by him. It is for this reason that the manuscript is a major addition to the Voltaire *corpus*.

The manuscript before us is valuable also in determining the extent of Voltaire's influence over and part in Frederick's poetry. In the most recent study of the king's verse, the author remarks that Voltaire did not consider himself above correcting the grammar or style (*sic*, 'and style' is clearly intended) of Frederick's verse.[1] And again: 'We cannot yet fully determine how great a part Voltaire had in the form and style of Frederick's poems.'[2] This is only partly true, for a collation of the passages quoted in Voltaire's letters to the crown prince and the king with the same passages as they appear in Frederick's published works yield an ample harvest of evidence. And so far as style is concerned it is obvious that Frederick deliberately modelled himself chiefly on Voltaire and Boileau: the echoes and even the direct imitations are numerous. Compare, for instance, in book iv of the *Art de la guerre*, the lines

> Tilly les endormit dans les bras du repos;
> Morphée avait sur eux répandu ses pavots,

with ii. 179–80 of the *Henriade*:

> Coligny languissait dans les bras du repos,
> Et le sommeil trompeur lui versait ses pavots,

the second line of which is in its turn an echo of Boileau (*Lutrin*, ii. 104):

> Et toujours le sommeil lui verse ses pavots.

However, we now have a definite and substantial body of evidence, concerning this one poem at least, showing that out of 1,600 lines over 300 are entirely by Voltaire, and that a good many more have been directly amended or influenced by him.

Before proceeding to a brief examination of the commentary, it may be noted in passing that Frederick studied Voltaire's

[1] Jagdhuhn, p. 138.    [2] Ibid., p. 164.

notes in the spirit of an uninspired schoolboy: where the master suggests an alternative the pupil usually adopts it word for word; where an actual form of words is not provided the indications given are followed as closely as possible; it is seldom that any changes are made other than those suggested by Voltaire, though he by no means exhausted the defects, even the mechanical ones, of the text before him. The only major case in which Frederick ignored Voltaire's advice was in respect of the conception and structure of the last book. There can be no doubt that the master's very severe strictures on that book are perfectly justified, but if they had been adopted the entire book would have had to be recast, and evidently the king could not face that.

Voltaire's remarks on the king's performance by no means represent the 'critique douce et civile' invited by Frederick in his letter of 13 February 1749. On the contrary, they are sharp in tone; little effort has been made to envelop them in compensatory compliments; the ardour of the critic carries him along, he does not hesitate to tell his royal pupil that passages of his work are bad, ridiculous, burlesque, comic, low, grotesque, and so on. And this although Voltaire was at this time in the king's bad books owing to the Hirschell affair. Those biographers who think that Voltaire was too profuse in his flattery of the king will have to revise their views when they read the barely disguised sarcasms with which he belabours Frederick in these notes, more particularly at the beginning of book vi. Indeed, as I hope to show in a future volume of the *Correspondence*, it is not impossible that the freedom with which Voltaire expresses himself here was a major cause of Frederick's temporary hatred for him: it was probably on reading Voltaire's commentary that the king began to feel that he had pretty well squeezed the orange.

Voltaire's notes fall into three categories: (1) corrections of historic details, and other facts; (2) corrections of grammatic details, construction, quantity, accord; (3) notes on vocabulary, meaning, and poetics generally.

On the first group there is nothing particular to remark, except to note, as always, how extremely well-informed and well-read Voltaire was: for it is rather surprising that he should have been able to spot mistakes in Frederick's history, as when he corrects 'fuit et passe le Rhin' to 'fuit jusqu'au bord du Rhin' (vi. 10. A). He objects when the king refers to the Graces yielding to the Loves, as described by Ovid, because neither Ovid nor anyone else ever said anything of the sort (i. 3. D).

The grammatical corrections are not of special interest: Frederick's French was technically pretty good, spelling apart, but it is not surprising that he should occasionally have confused his genders and tenses, and failed to spot some intransitive verbs and aspirated h's.

It is with Voltaire's literary comments that we come to the heart of the matter. Let us briefly sum up his views, as expressed in the manuscript before us, with a few illustrative examples.

*Energy*

One of Voltaire's major objections to the king's poem is that he finds many passages too languid, vague, imprecise, in structure as well as imagery. This appears to be due to padding (see below); the use of too many long words ('en général les mots trop longs et composés de syllabes maigres et sourdes doivent s'éviter, surtout en rimes') (ii. 6. D); the use of participles (e.g. ii. 11. BBB) and of imperfect verbs (iii. 10. A); and the insufficient breaking-up of meaning within the lines. An almost perfect example of all this is provided by the very first lines contributed by Voltaire to the poem (i. 1. CD): not great poetry, to be sure, but this 'simplicité majestueuse' can be read with interest, and without the boredom inspired by Frederick's woolly verse.

A little later the king, guided by Voltaire, transforms the feeble 'Que l'exercice enseigne aux soldats commençants' into 'Que le dieu des guerriers enseigne à ses enfants' (i. 4. gg).

3. Houdon's signature on the statue

And in general, whenever Voltaire rewrites a passage of several lines, an increase of energy, of muscular tone, is immediately perceived.

## *Vocabulary*

'Cherchons toujours des termes pittoresques, des tours neufs, un choix d'expressions heureuses' (ii. 7. d) well sums up Voltaire's views on poetic vocabulary. Here is one of the chief secrets of his miraculous style: his wonderfully sensitive ear for the slightest shades of meaning.

Many of Voltaire's comments on Frederick's choice of words refer to matters of good or bad usage as established by tradition. Although the king was well if not deeply read in French literature he was rather insensitive here. Thus, when Frederick apostrophizes (i. 2) the

génie heureux
Qui sur notre salut veillez du haut des cieux,

Voltaire rightly points out that 'salut' has theological overtones inappropriate in the context. However, by suggesting 'les Prussiens' for 'notre salut' Voltaire seems to have made matters worse: for who is this 'génie heureux' who watches over the Prussians from on high? Again Voltaire points out that 'on manie un cheval, on gouverne des chevaux' (i. 13. *). 'Sublime, tout court, ne se dit guères que du style' (iii. 1. A).

Equally often Voltaire points out the use of inappropriate or simply inaccurate words. Thus he explains (i. 2. D) that frightful sights, murderous furies, and bloody death cannot be said to 'engloutir' mankind. When Frederick writes of the enemy: 'Quelque arrogant qu'il soit', Voltaire states that only conduct and speech can be arrogant; the enemy is passionate, eager, audacious (ii. 7. c). 'Noirceurs' is not the right term for the excesses committed by soldiers, says Voltaire, because it implies premeditated crimes (iv. 8. c). In describing the art of choosing one's terrain, and the like, Frederick writes: 'Par ces enchantements le destin se corrige.' On this Voltaire comments that 'enchantement' is not the right word, since the king is teaching a skill (ii. 8. A).

Sometimes Voltaire's niceness in such matters induces him to make what appear at first sight to be perhaps over-subtle distinctions, as when he finds (i. 3. *) the word 'frénésie' barely suitable for an ode and not at all for a didactic poem. However, Voltaire does not mean this to be taken literally: what he objects to is that the narrator makes himself 'représenter, plein de ma frénésie', which is clearly out of character. In short, it is not the word Voltaire objects to but the way in which it is used.

Another frequent defect pointed out in the commentary is the repetition of a given word soon after its first occurrence (e.g. i. 7. BB); but Voltaire overlooked some of these, and even aggravated the offence, such as it is (v. 5. B, note 1).

Here as elsewhere Voltaire does not hesitate to mingle a little satire with his criticisms. Thus, when Frederick apostrophizes the addressee of his poem, who at this point is a general, 'Si vous voulez briller en commandant l'armée...', Voltaire comments that it is not a question here of shining but of assuring the welfare of an army (ii. 3. C).

### Correct imagery and descriptions

The beginning of the *Art* is a confused mixture of straight narrative and metaphor. Voltaire points out that there is no art of hurling the thunder and that thunder does not sit too well with arms, horses, and cannon (i. 1. CD). In Frederick's typically vague description of the fountain of Marly, he refers to its 'ressorts, les uns qui foulent l'eau, les autres l'aspirant'. Voltaire points out that springs do neither the one nor the other (i. 6. A). He objects to 'décrets' as applied to the laws of Rome (i. 11. B).

One cannot speak of a torrent of hail, says Voltaire, because a torrent flows, and hail does not (ii. 6. A). When Frederick writes that a

> nuage sombre, obscurcissant sa gloire,
> Vint effacer son nom du temple de mémoire,

Voltaire finds insupportable the notion of a cloud 'qui vient dans un temple effacer un nom' (iv. 9. B). He certainly does not exaggerate when he finds 'avare de pudeur' grotesque (iv. 12. A).

As so often in Voltaire's critical writings, his objections, as we have already noted, go deeper than surface poetics. Thus, when Frederick writes of the soldiers who in winter await 'du riant printemps l'agréable venue', by which he means that they are preparing for the next campaign, Voltaire reminds him that he is not writing an eclogue: 'le printemps est alors funeste. Il me semble que cela n'a jamais été dit et doit l'être.' Again, when Frederick refers to the 'foudre des héros' falling on the throne, Voltaire dryly remarks that cannon-balls fall first on armies and ramparts (i. 4. A).

### Nobility, originality, grace

Yet it is not enough to be exact, 'il faut de l'élégance' (ii. 6. E). As Voltaire himself admirably puts it, 'le mérite de la poésie et surtout de la poésie didactique ne consiste-il pas à dire singulièrement les choses communes?' (i. 4. E). Again and again he objects to Frederick's use of flat, commonplace, prosaic words. (The truth is, of course—it must be repeated, for Voltaire sometimes loses sight of the fact—that it is not the words themselves that are objectionable, but the way in which they are used, their relative weight in the line, the words they are given as neighbours.) Voltaire's highest praise for a passage is that it is expressed 'noblement et avec justesse' (i. 8. BB).

Voltaire finds 'dieu de la guerre' and 'lancer le tonnerre' too vague, too commonplace for the invocation at the beginning of the poem. 'Tout nu', in describing the frolics of the Loves, is not considered sufficiently noble (i. 3. D). 'Dressé', as applied to the training of a soldier, is too trivial: 'encore une fois le grand secret est d'ennoblir ces détails' (i. 6. BB). '[A] faire la retraite' is rejected as too prosaic, and is replaced by 'le force à la retraite' (i. 7. BB).

'Les affaires', in 'Quelquefois le hasard fait changer les

affaires', says Voltaire, 'est bien loin d'être du style poétique, il
ne serait pas même ici du style de prose' (ii. 7. A). Voltaire does
not consider it noble or poetic to refer to Alexander the Great
or Scipio the African: 'il faut ce me semble désigner ces gens-là
plutôt que les nommer', and he proposes 'Le vainqueur des
Persans, le vainqueur de Pompée' (iii. 6. B). He objects to the
word 'volume' applied by Frederick to his poem. A poet is
inspired, he should not know that there are such things as
printing-presses (v. 1. A).

Frederick sometimes joins bathos to lowness: Voltaire tells
him that 'après avoir dit *si vous aspirez à être un fameux capitaine*
on attend quelque autre chose que de distinguer un cul pointu
d'avec une belle croupe de cheval' (i. 8. BB).

### Rhyme, assonance

Frederick's skill was not such as to give rise to interesting
notes by Voltaire on a high technical level. That 'savoir les
devoirs' is a 'consonance dure' (i. 7. AA) is obvious. When
Voltaire finds 'charge' rhyming with the same word he exclaims 'désinence plus dure' (i. 7. AA): but surely that is not
quite what he means?

Voltaire does not like alliteration: in 'Affrontent les efforts
des vents', which strikes one as a pretty good effort for
Frederick, he replaces 'efforts' by 'assauts' (i. 7. C).

He objects also to the use of technical words as rhymes:
'c'est là où le poète doit chercher des ressources de génie pour
peindre singulièrement les choses communes' (ii. 3. BBB). In
general, Voltaire is particularly severe on the misuse of technical terms (e.g. iv. 7. A–B; and *passim*).

### Padding

Frederick opens his poem with an introductory address to
himself written in the person of a 'généreux soldat' (himself
again? Voltaire very properly objected, i. 1. B, to this epithet),

who proposes to instruct the addressee in the art of hurling the thunder in order that he may learn to defend and judge the state. Voltaire points out (i. 1. A) that the lessons of a soldier do not teach him to judge [a nation]. Frederick of course knew this: the words 'et juger' are meaningless, they are in fact padding to fill out the metre.

Similarly Voltaire shows Frederick how to plug an empty line with a concrete form of words instead of a mere 'vers de remplissage' (i. 5. cc). 'Un peu chevillard' [< cheville, 'padding'], says Voltaire of another line. 'Fuyez les idées étrangères, dit Locke, excellent précepte en poésie comme en prose' (ii. 2. E).

There is not infrequently an overlap between these subjects, as when Voltaire gives five reasons for objecting to one short phrase (ii. 1. c). Again at the beginning of i. 2 Frederick writes:

> Mais ne présumez point que...
> Je séduise vos sens par un faux point d'honneur.
> Ah! plutôt qu'Attila vous servît de modèle.

Voltaire is obliged to point out that 'point d'honneur' is prosaic, that it is more suited to a duel than to war, and that in any case Attila did not make war on a point of honour.

It must be owned that Voltaire's comments are not always easy to follow, though of course *de gustibus*.... Take this passage (iv. 11. N.B.): 'Savez vous les vers qui m'ont le plus touché dans tout cela? c'est

> Dans un asile saint, inutile en ce temps,
> Egorgent sans pitié trois cent vieillards tremblants.

C'est que cela est vrai. Rien n'est beau que le vrai, et cet *asile inutile* est admirable.' Voltaire was neither the first nor the last to urge that 'Beauty is truth, truth beauty', but if his dictum is interpreted in the light of what he himself considered to be poetic beauty, it is difficult indeed to share his admiration for this couplet. 'Inutile en ce temps' appears to be crude tautology, since if a massacre takes place within its walls, the 'asile' is clearly 'inutile'. These words are not merely padding, but padding for the rhyme. Is not 'Egorgent sans pitié' distinctly trite? And is not 'trois cent' at best prosaic?

Incidentally, the second of these lines is largely Voltaire's; Frederick actually wrote: 'Egorgent sans remords trois cent bourgeois tremblants', which is even worse, since remorse cannot come until after the deed, and the social status of the victims is neither poetic nor relevant.

# Voltaire's Love-Letters[1]

*to Nancy Mitford*

BEAUMARCHAIS, Condorcet, and their associates assembled nearly 5,000 of Voltaire's letters in the Kehl edition published a few years after the great man's death. A century later the number had been doubled. And about ten years ago, when I completed my first inventory of the surviving letters, I was staggered to find that the figure had increased to 16,000. Then more and more series and single letters were traced, several important collections mislaid or stolen during the Second World War were recovered, private collections and public archives yielded up unrecorded treasures (such as the hundreds of letters in the private collection of the Queen of the Netherlands—graciously made available on Her Majesty's initiative), others (not yet all) finally agreed to allow access to their manuscripts, further letters were found in obscure publications, and by the time I started the publication of *Voltaire's Correspondence* in 1953 the number had risen to 18,000. The production of successive volumes has served only to widen the flood. Today I have 19,000 letters on file, about 90 per cent. of them in manuscript or photocopy—and still they pour in.

It is known that Voltaire's niece, Mme Denis, was his residuary legatee, and that on his death she hastened to sell his library and papers to Catherine II. At first placed in the Hermitage, they are now piously preserved in the Saltuikov-Shchedrin library at Leningrad—and I am happy to be able to say that microfilms of the manuscripts are now beginning to come through. The manuscripts in Voltaire's library at Leningrad were inventoried by Caussy in 1913, and an examination

[1] First printed in the *Times Literary Supplement*, 30 August 1957.

of his calendar yields valuable information of more than one kind, both positive and negative. The point that has always struck me most is the complete absence of true personal and family papers. It was thus evident that Mme Denis held back some of Voltaire's files, and as there had not been the slightest sign of them since his death it looked as though they had been destroyed, like his letters to Mme Du Châtelet.

However, just before the Second World War a group of Voltaire's letters to Mme Denis came on the market, and were published under the title of *Lettres d'Alsace*. Unfortunately no information whatever was given by the editor as to the whereabouts and provenance of these letters. And in any case they threw no light on Voltaire's own files. They did, however, revive hopes that Mme Denis's papers, at least, had survived. But when inquiries were resumed after the war, not only could no new papers be found but even the originals of the *Lettres d'Alsace* had disappeared. These last have finally been traced; they are in the possession of Mr. D. N. Heineman,[1] an American collector, who has not only safeguarded their future but has most kindly furnished me with a microfilm of the whole series.

As for the rest of Mme Denis's papers, this much was discovered: Mme Denis (*née* Marie Louise Mignot) was the elder daughter of Voltaire's sister Catherine Mignot (*née* Arouet), who had also a younger daughter, Marie Elisabeth. Mme Denis (who ought really to be called Mme Duvivier, for she remarried after Voltaire's death) had no children, but her sister married first Nicolas Joseph de Dompierre de Fontaine, and after his death the Marquis de Florian. By her first marriage she had a son, the future *président* Alexandre de Dompierre d'Hornoy (1742–1828), who became the residuary legatee of Mme Denis on her death in 1790. From him the family heirlooms passed successively to his son Victor and his grandson Albéric, who had only two daughters. One of these entered a convent; the other, Léonie, married Ambroise de Glos, whose grandson, Guy de Glos, is today the proprietor of the

[1] Who died as the proofs of these pages were being corrected.

château d'Hornoy built by the *président*. (A fascinating detail: among the other descendants of Voltaire's sister was Father Pierre Teilhard de Chardin.)

Through these successive generations the papers that passed from Mme Denis to her nephew remained intact until about 1935, when they were sold. One small part of them came to light—these are the *Lettres d'Alsace*—but no trace could be found of the others, though some idea of their nature had been gleaned from the family: they included, in fact, the bulk of the personal papers, not only of Voltaire, but also of Mme Denis and of the *président* d'Hornoy, including hundreds of Voltaire letters. These papers recently reappeared, and all the Voltaire letters came into my hands. The rest of the material, alas, will be thrown on the market and dispersed unless a library or collector comes forward very quickly.[1]

Among the Voltaire letters one series is of outstanding importance. This precious group consists of a continuous sequence of 142 letters (written in 1742–1750) from Voltaire to Mme Denis—and what letters! In Voltaire's correspondence there are many letters addressed to the women he loved: but though they are the letters of a lover, they can hardly be described as love-letters, not even those addressed to Countess Bentinck, which I had the privilege of publishing for the first time in *Voltaire's Correspondence* thanks to the kindness of [the late] Louis C. G. Clarke. If those were a revelation what can be said of these?

It was clear from the *Lettres d'Alsace* that Voltaire's feelings for his favourite niece had gone well beyond avuncular affection, but it seemed as though their affair had been a short-lived interlude, precipitated by their detention together in Frankfurt by order of Frederick II. The letters now found reveal the truth, which is very different. They are real love-letters—and it would be idle to hope that those written to Mme Du Châtelet

---

[1] Nearly the whole is now in the collections of the Institut et Musée Voltaire, except the letters to Mme Denis and the *président* d'Hornoy, which are in the Pierpont Morgan library.

may still turn up. Another remarkable feature of these letters to his niece is the fact that the greater proportion of them is in Italian.

When his sister died Voltaire was in England, and could not behave as the good family man he was. There is evidence, however, to show that he took a lively interest in his two nieces, and when their father in turn died Voltaire made himself responsible for them, invited them to Cirey, gave them money and presents, and endowed them generously on their marriages. Marie Louise was difficult to please, and finally made her own choice, after rejecting several matches proposed by Voltaire, who, with rare tolerance, quite approved: 'I want her to be happy in her fashion, not in mine.' The young couple owed their prosperity and advancement to Voltaire's influence, but in 1744 young Denis died. His widow, now aged thirty-two, returned to Paris, and a few months later her uncle joined her there, at the beginning of that most uncharacteristic period of his life: that of Voltaire the courtier. When uncle and niece met they seem to have fallen at once into each other's arms, and family affection turned overnight into love.

Until then, Voltaire addressed Mme Denis as 'ma chère nièce' and concluded 'with fond kisses' ('je vous embrasse tendrement'); but in the first surviving letter after his arrival in Paris (31 August 1744) he begins 'mia carissima' and ends 'You are my whole family, my sole friend, my treasure [il mio bene], and my only hope'. He invites her to the theatre, the opera, the ballet, to his room in the palace, near 'the most stinking shit-hole in Versailles', to see the bonfire at the place de Grève, to dinner. She is the first to hear of his triumphs at court, of the places given to him by the king, his election to the Academy, announcements always overlaid by an obvious disgust with all the things he is obliged to do to gain and keep the favour of a monarch who detested him. There is a remarkable letter filled with sarcasms about 'his most gracious majesty'.

Above all, these letters are shot through with constant

protestations of love, expressions of despair at the enforced separation imposed by his duties at Versailles, and his constant bad health. 'Ah, how many days before I see you again!' ... 'If only we could live together in one house.' ... 'If only our fates were different and we could always be together.' ... And although it is obvious that Voltaire, that least self-revelatory of all great writers, found it difficult to let himself go, often strong passion—or, let me say it plainly, lust—breaks through. 'I kiss you a thousand times. My soul embraces yours, my prick and my heart are enamoured of you. I embrace your pretty bottom and all your adorable person'; this will suffice as a specimen.

Perhaps most fascinating in this correspondence, as in that with Countess Bentinck, though the tone is very different, are the little notes dashed off and sent round by hand:

My dear, my dear, health and I have sworn an eternal divorce. I wanted to go to see you, and I am going to bed. But I swear by all the saints and by your charms that I will see you tomorrow if I am able to go out. Goodbye, dear one.

I am obliged to go out but I shall be back about six o'clock. I will wait for you, my dear soul. We will reason together about a thousand things. My health makes me suffer cruelly, but your tenderness cures me. I kiss you a thousand times.

Incidentally, 'ragioneremo insieme', in the private language of the lovers, like the 'successful' in the next note, does not mean quite what it appears to mean.

You have written a marvellously successful letter. I want to thank you for it, and if you are alone I will come to dine with the most amiable woman in Paris, but really, I have to starve to death in order to live. How is my dear one?

Mme Denis endorsed this note: 'I reproach my heart.'

And so it went on, with unabated love and tenderness—all this unique in Voltaire's surviving correspondence, for his tenderness was usually reserved for wretches like Thieriot—year after year, until the miserable death in 1749 of Emilie Du

Châtelet, whom Voltaire would not have left for the world. The tragedy that should have opened the way to a new life, the longed-for beginning, was in fact the opposite. Voltaire returned to Paris, set up house with his niece, but then decided to go to Prussia, where Mme Denis refused to follow him. She rejoined him when he escaped from Frederick, only to be imprisoned in Frankfurt, and there, briefly, Voltaire forgot Mme Bentinck. But we now know that what I, for one, took to be a brief *passade* was in fact the last flicker of a fire that had burnt for nearly ten years. It is true that later, as he approached Geneva, Voltaire again took his niece to live with him; it is true that he still loved her, and in fact later letters show that his devotion never entirely waned; but it was not again as it had been in those years at Paris and Versailles.

Of course Voltaire did not cease to be himself even when writing love-letters to his niece. And so these contain long disquisitions on his plays, including the writing of *Sémiramis* and *La Mort de César*; on Crébillon, Marmontel, and others; on life at the court of Stanislas; and a hundred other things. There is not the slightest reference, however, any more here than in his other correspondence, to the most important literary event of this period, the creation of the *conte philosophique*: yet it was at this time that he wrote *Memnon*, the first version of *Zadig*.

# Emilie Du Châtelet: Portrait of an Unknown Woman[1]

*to the memory of Count Charles de Breteuil*

## I

THESE few pages do not constitute a new biography: they merely contain a few notes designed to draw attention to new elements in the life of Mme Du Châtelet, that great unknown, whose real biography remains to be written, in spite of the many works that have been devoted to one who would have been rare in any age, and was unique in the eighteenth century.

## II

Gildhuin, first Count of Breteuil in the Beauvaisis, was, through his union with Ermeline, whom he married in 1020, the ancestor of Pierre Le Tonnelier, who was alive in 1378. From this time we can trace the descent in the direct male line down to our own day. Few families can claim such antiquity. Pierre was followed in turn by Thibault (dead in 1420), Pierre (living in 1433), Henry (living in 1472), Jean (living in 1481), Claude (married in 1502), and Jean (married in 1536). The third of this Jean's five children was Claude Le Tonnelier de Breteuil, lord of Breteuil (?1540–1608), secretary of the king's chamber. His first-born, also Claude, became director of finances (1580–1653). His son Louis (1609–85) was Intendant of Paris, controller-general of finances, and marquis; he married Chrétienne

[1] Extract from the preliminary notes to my edition of the *Lettres de la Marquise Du Châtelet* (Institut et Musée Voltaire: Geneva 1958).

Le Court (1616–1707), who bore him many children, including Louis Nicolas Le Tonnelier de Breteuil, Baron de Preuilly, who became successively reader in ordinary to the king, envoy extraordinary to the princes of Italy, and chief of protocol. He was born on 14 September 1648, and died on 24 March 1728.

He was a man, Saint-Simon tells us, in language which in spite of its usual malice does not wholly distort the truth,

who was not lacking in wit, but who had a passion for the court, for ministers, for men of position or in favour, and above all for acquiring money in disputes by promising his protection. People put up with him, and made fun of him. He hung around a great deal at M. de Pontchartrain's, where Caumartin, his friend and relative, had introduced him. Although respectful enough, he was clearly very satisfied with his own abilities, and people liked to tease him.

This portrait needs to be modified by the baron's own memoirs, which have never been published in their entirety but can be seen in manuscript in the city library of Rouen.

On 3 August 1679 the Baron de Breteuil, already related, as Saint-Simon says, to the Caumartins (one of his grandmothers was a Le Fèvre de Caumartin), married Marie Anne Le Fèvre de Caumartin. He was soon left a widower, and on 15 April 1697 married Gabrielle Anne de Froulay, who died on 4 August 1740. Of this second marriage was born in Paris, on 17 December 1706, Gabrielle Emilie Le Tonnelier de Breteuil. All we know of her childhood comes from the accounts given by Voltaire. First, in his *Eloge historique de madame la marquise Du Châtelet* (Moland, xxiii. 520), he writes:

From her earliest youth she nourished her mind on the best authors in more than one language. She began a translation of the *Aeneid*, and the passages I have seen show her characteristic magnanimity. She afterwards learned Italian and English. Tasso and Milton were as familiar to her as Virgil. She did not get so far in Spanish, because she was told that there was really only one book in that language, and that a frivolous one.

And in his *Mémoires* Voltaire adds (Moland, i. 7): 'Her father, Baron de Breteuil, had her taught Latin, which she knew as well as Mme Dacier; she knew by heart the finest passages of Horace, Virgil, and Lucretius. All the philosophical works of Cicero were familiar to her. Her strongest inclination was towards mathematics and metaphysics.'

What Voltaire says does not necessarily derive from what the marquise may have told him, because being himself an intimate of the Caumartins and the Baron de Breteuil, he no doubt knew all these details at first hand. But this is not all there is to be said. Mme Du Châtelet's passion for music, above all for singing, indicates that her education in this direction also must have been very thorough.

### III

On 12 June 1725 the young woman, not yet nineteen, was married to Florent Claude, Marquis Du Châtelet-Lomont, a family of nobler connexions but less antiquity than the Le Tonneliers. Florent Claude was born on 7 April 1695 at Namur, of which his father was governor. He entered the army and served in several campaigns. At the time of his marriage he held the rank of colonel, and to mark the occasion was made governor of the town, castle, and keep of Semur. He was not a man of great distinction, but he was mild, intelligent, and easy to get on with, and his wife never felt anything but respect and friendship towards him.

On 29 September 1725 the young couple made their triumphal entry into Semur, with a procession, banquet, and the rest. All the details can be found in an interesting pamphlet by Ledeuil-d'Enquin. On 30 June 1726 Françoise Gabrielle Pauline was born, who in 1743 married Alfonso Caraffa, Duke of Montenero; and on 20 November 1727 Louis Marie Florent, destined to become Duc Du Châtelet, ambassador to the court of St. James's, and one of the first victims of the Revolution. Having fulfilled her basic duties to her children, the marquise accompanied her husband to Paris in 1730, and probably paid only brief visits after that to her beautiful house at Semur.

In Paris, as was almost obligatory, Mme Du Châtelet took lovers, of whom the first may have been Louis Vincent, Marquis de Guébriant. The account that the Comte de Maurepas gives of this liaison seems probable enough when one reads the marquise's love-letters. But it must be remembered that Maurepas hated Voltaire all his life, and through him all his friends. This is what Maurepas says in his *Mémoires* (Paris 1792, iv. 173):

The Marquise Du Châtelet, daughter of the Baron de Breteuil, desperate at being abandoned by the Marquis de Guébriant, whom she idolized, wrote him a letter full of eternal farewells, saying she wished to die now that he was dead to her. Guébriant, who knew her to be capable of extremes, rushed to her house, and being refused entry, broke in, flew to her apartments, and found her stretched out, having swallowed a dose of opium sufficient to kill her. He called for assistance, and saved her life, but finding herself unable to bind him to her in spite of this proof of her love, she consoled herself with various others.

Raynal gives a similar account of this incident (*Correspondance littéraire*, i. 365–6).

Of these 'various others' only the Duc de Richelieu and Maupertuis are known, though no precise details have been discovered. We now have the letters which the marquise wrote to them at a later date, and these leave no doubt about the nature of her relations with them. Apparently the liaison of Mme Du Châtelet with Richelieu was never renewed, though several letters show that there was a time when she would have had no objection. That the liaison with Maupertuis was not discontinued even during the first days of her love for Voltaire can hardly fail to shock even her most indulgent admirers, and reveals a certain lack of delicacy in the character of a woman otherwise so sensitive. Later, during a journey or probably during several journeys to the Low Countries, there comes a

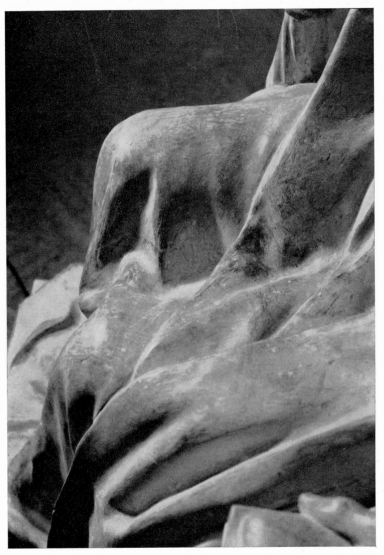

4. Detail of the statue, showing the marks of the sculptor's tool

brief affair with her counsellor Charlier. For the rest, information is lacking for the period preceding the fatal encounter
with Saint-Lambert.

## IV

It was probably in the spring of 1733 that Voltaire renewed
acquaintance with Mme Du Châtelet. She was twenty-seven,
he thirty-nine. He was famous, and attractive. At first there
were discreet foursomes with the Duchesse de Saint-Pierre and
the Comte de Forcalquier (Best. 658):

> Je reçus chez moi l'autre jour
> De déesses un couple aimable
> Conduit par le dieu d'amour;
> Du paradis l'heureux séjour,
> N'a jamais rien eu de semblable. . . .

> (There came to me the other day,
> Conducted by the god of love,
> Two goddesses both fair and gay.
> Eden in our first parents' stay
> Had no joys fit to rank above.)

He apologizes for not having been able to ask them to dine
with him:

> Ciel! que j'entendrais s'écrier
> Mariamne ma cuisinière,
> Si la duchesse de Saint-Pierre,
> Du Châtelet et Forcalquier
> Venaient souper dans ma tanière!

> (Lord, I could hear Maria say,
> Who can the master have in there?
> I'd die if Madame de Saint-Pierre,
> The Count, and Madame Du Châtelet
> Should stay and sup in such a lair!)

But events soon forced the lovers' hands. Voltaire had arranged
the marriage between Richelieu and the Princesse de Guise.

Both he and Mme Du Châtelet went to the ceremony, but no sooner had he arrived at Montjeu than he learned that the king had issued a warrant for his arrest because of the *Lettres philosophiques*, and he fled to Cirey. He set about adding a new wing to the château, and refurnishing and redecorating all the rest. He was soon joined by Mme Du Châtelet, and during the autumn of 1734 began the famous retreat of love and learning.

## V

I have quoted Saint-Simon's portrait of the Baron de Breteuil. It has a pendant in the portrait painted of his daughter by a pen no less caustic than the duke's and far more witty. Here is the description by Mme Du Deffand, in the authentic text, taken from the manuscript now in the possession of Mr. Wilmarth S. Lewis:

Imagine a tall, gaunt woman with a high complexion, a thin face, and a sharp nose. Such is the aspect of the lovely Emilie, an aspect with which she is so satisfied that she spares no effort to set it off—curls, bobbles, jewels, beads, masses of everything. But as she is trying to be beautiful in spite of nature, and magnificent in spite of fortune, she is obliged to sacrifice necessity to luxury, and do without such trifles as underwear.

She is by nature quite intelligent, but the desire to appear more so has led her to prefer the most abstract sciences to more agreeable studies. She thinks by this singularity to win greater reputation, and a more marked superiority over all other women.

Nor does she content herself with this ambition. She must also be a princess. And she has become one, not by the grace of God, nor by favour of the king, but thanks to herself. It is with this as with all her other follies: people have got into the habit of regarding her as a make-believe princess, and forgotten that she is a woman of rank.

Our fine lady works so hard to appear what she is not that no one remembers what she really is. Perhaps even her faults are unnatural, and belong rather to her pretensions than to her: her lack of consideration to her ambition to be a princess, her brusqueness to her desire to be thought learned, and her skittishness to her pose of being a pretty woman.

However celebrated Mme Du Châtelet might be, she could never be satisfied unless she was a celebrity, and this is what she attained by becoming the declared lover of M. de Voltaire. It is he who lends lustre to her life, and to him that she will owe her immortality.

There are certain portraits whose subtlety and penetration absolve them from the requirements of objective accuracy. But this is not the case with the portrait drawn by the wretched Mme Du Deffand, whose boredom and cynicism, in her worst moods, left their traces on all she touched. It may well be that Mme Du Chatelet was a tall woman, but it is impossible to be certain. It is impossible to be certain about this point in the case of Voltaire himself: some eye-witness descriptions say he was very tall, others maintain that he was very short. It is hardly likely that the marquise was gaunt: everything about her life, and her portraits, give a different impression. A high complexion?—yes. Thin face? Sharp nose? Everything is relative, but even if Mme Du Châtelet's nose was perhaps rather long, no authentic portrait proves that it was sharp. As for the bobbles and all the rest of it, the marquise was the first to acknowledge her weakness for this sort of thing, and Voltaire teased her affectionately about it. That the Le Tonneliers and the Du Châtelets were both families of modest means, and that it pleased Voltaire to surround his mistress with every possible comfort and even luxury—that may have been a reason for jealousy in Mme Du Deffand, but it was not a crime.

Besides, it is very probable that the expensive gifts that Voltaire lavished on Mme Du Châtelet were a delicate means of providing for her future. Here is an unpublished quatrain addressed to the marquise:

> Pardonne aux diamants qui forment la bordure
> D'un portrait de peu de valeur.
> Je n'ai pas mis tant d'art à te donner mon cœur:
> Il n'a pas besoin de parure.

> (Forgive the frame of precious stone
> That holds my portrait. When I sent

My heart to you, it came alone,
Having no need of ornament.)

And to the verses Voltaire added the significant words: 'Here is another bit in case of accidents.'

As for the luxury of the château itself, people have let themselves be led astray by the slightly vulgar pen of Mme de Graffigny. Let us listen rather to President Hénault's more sober account (9 July 1744; Best. 2789):

I called at Cirey also. It's a unique thing. There they both are, all alone, steeped in pleasures. One sits composing verses, the other drawing triangles. The house is built in the Romanesque style, with unusual splendour. Voltaire has an apartment ending in a gallery like the one you've seen in the picture of the *School of Athens* [i.e. the fresco by Raphael in the Stanza della Signatura], where there's a collection of instruments of all kinds—mathematical, physical, chemical, astronomical, mechanical, and so on, and in addition to all this, antique lacquers, glass, pictures, Dresden china, and so on. In short, you think you're dreaming.

All this is evidence of study and good taste rather than of luxury.

VI

As for what Mme Du Deffand says of the intelligence, education, and ambitions of Mme Du Châtelet, there is only one possible comment: she knew nothing about it, she was completely incapable of understanding. It is undeniable that Mme Du Châtelet's celebrity derives from her relationship with Voltaire. Yet it is not a question here of celebrity but of intrinsic qualities. It was not Voltaire's friendship that enabled her to do solid work in several fields, and to have a piece of research published by the Académie des Sciences; or to correspond for many years with some of the foremost men of science of the age; or to enter into public disputation with Mairan on the technical details of physics.

What exactly was the extent of Mme Du Châtelet's work and knowledge? In the field of physics and metaphysics, two

subjects closely linked in her mind, it is not impossible to arrive
at an accurate answer. It is true that anyone who wished to be
sceptical could allege that for the merits of her dissertation on
the nature of fire, and her *Institutions*, and the great commentary on Newton, she is indebted to Maupertuis, König, and
Clairault. I do not think this point of view can survive the
study of a large number of so far unpublished passages from
her letters to Maupertuis, and from newly discovered letters
to Bernoulli and Jurin. In these letters can be followed, even
through errors and technical insufficiencies, the thoughts of a
scientific mind which has grasped very firmly the fundamental
principles of physics and of the scientific method on which all
truth is based. In fact it is clear that Mme Du Châtelet was
capable of discussing the most abstract questions of physics
with intelligence and in a spirit of enlightened criticism. Nor
must it be forgotten that many of these letters were written
to men often said to have been her ghosts. It would have been
very silly to address them to people who would have known
very well that she was incapable of them.

And we must not forget, either, the by no means negligible
testimony of Diderot, who once said that he had had 'two happy
moments in his life', one of which was on receiving a letter
from Mme Du Châtelet (which has unfortunately been lost)
about his *Lettre sur les aveugles*.[1]

These views gain valuable confirmation from several manuscripts that have yet to be thoroughly studied. In September
1749 (Best. 3479) Voltaire wrote to the Comte d'Argental: 'I
have just re-read some very extensive material on metaphysics
which Mme Du Châtelet amassed with terrifying patience and
sagacity. . . . She had the genius of a Leibniz, and sensibility
as well.' What were these manuscripts? It is very difficult to say,
but I think it probable that Voltaire refers here to the commentary on Newton. However that may be, there exists in the
Bibliothèque nationale (Fr. 12265) the manuscript of the *Institutions physiques*. The greater part of it is in the Marquise's own

---

[1] See Diderot, *Correspondance*, ed. Georges Roth (Paris 1955), i. 115.

hand, with a certain number of pages written by an amanuensis, and some heavily corrected proofs. A collation of this manuscript with the published version sheds a good deal of light on Mme Du Châtelet's learning.

Even more striking is another manuscript now also in the Bibliothèque nationale (Fr. 12266–8). This is the work to which Mme Du Châtelet devoted her last years, sending the manuscript to the king's library on the very day she died: 'Mathematical principles of natural philosophy by Monsieur Newton translated into French by Madame la Marquise du Chastellet with a commentary on those propositions which relate to the system of the world.' These three volumes, commentary as well as text, are entirely in the marquise's hand, including the diagrams and mathematical calculations.

Volume ix of Voltaire's manuscripts, which Mme Denis lost no time in selling to Catherine II almost as soon as her uncle was dead, contains more than 300 sheets of manuscript by the marquise. As far as one can judge from Caussy's rather cursory inventory, this volume contains not only the published works of Mme Du Châtelet, but also notes on Descartes, and others on his physics, her reflections, and an essay on government—historical, political, and religious, ancient and modern (but is this not more likely to be an abstract?). The fragment on free-will that is also included is not by Mme Du Châtelet but by Voltaire (see Ira O. Wade, *Studies on Voltaire*, pp. 92–108). Lastly, there is a dissertation on Elia and Enoch (by Boulanger), an exposition of the doctrine of the Gallican church on the claims of the court of Rome, and a manuscript entitled 'Religion, par Dumarsais'.

So it cannot any longer be maintained that Mme Du Châtelet's scientific and scholarly pursuits were no more than eccentricity or pastime. She was surely thinking of herself when she said, in her *Réflexions sur le bonheur*: 'I have said that the love of study is the passion most necessary to our happiness. It is a sure resource against misfortune, a source of inexhaustible pleasure.' One may even wonder, in the light of what we know, and of Mr. Wade's two books, whether Mme Du Châtelet did not perhaps have more influence on certain of Voltaire's ideas and preoccupations than he ever had on her. Here, as in other spheres, the personality of the marquise has been too often, and unjustly, confused with that of her lover.

## VII

How did Voltaire and Mme Du Châtelet come to be separated from each other? One would have to be quite lacking in historical sense to reproach the marquise for not having given Voltaire her exclusive devotion, even in the first years of their love. There were very few women in the eighteenth century who limited themselves to one lover at a time. Of course husbands don't count. If Marie Leszczinska had wished to surround herself with virtuous women, she would have led an even more solitary existence than she did. But people have often found it astonishing and even reprehensible that Mme Du Châtelet should have abandoned a man like Voltaire for a man like Saint-Lambert. We have recently learned that the truth is very different, and we now realize how faithful an account Mme Du Châtelet herself gives us of the matter in her *Réflexions sur le bonheur*. They were published in 1796, but no one, apparently, has troubled to read them with true understanding. Here is a moving extract:

God bestowed on me one of those loving and unchanging hearts that can neither disguise nor moderate their passions, that know neither weariness nor satiety, and have the steadfastness that resists all, even the knowledge of being loved no longer. But for ten years I was happy in the love of him who had conquered my heart, and I passed those ten years in the closest intimacy with him, without the least moment of weariness or disgust. When age, illness, and perhaps also surfeit of pleasure,[1] lessened his desire, it was a long time before

[1] To the many criticisms, some valid, some not, which have been levelled at Voltaire, a new one has recently been added, astonishing in its foolish ignorance: it is alleged in the *Progrès médical* of 24 March 1956 (p. 133), and again in the issue of 10 February 1957 (p. 69), that Voltaire 'was impotent from youth'.

I perceived it. I loved enough for two. My whole life was passed beside him, and my heart, knowing no suspicion, rejoiced in the pleasure of loving and the illusion of thinking I was loved. Now, it is true, that happy state is lost to me, and the loss has cost me many tears.

Terrible shocks are needed to break such bonds; the wound in my heart bled for a long time. I had cause for complaint, and I forgave everything. I was sufficiently just to realize that perhaps mine was the only heart in the world so unchanging as to annihilate the power of time; that if age and illness had not quite extinguished his desires they might perhaps have still belonged to me, and love would have brought him back to me; and that, if his heart was no longer capable of love, he held me in the tenderest friendship, and would have given his life for me. The certainty that his desire and passion could never return, for I knew that to be outside the possibilities of nature, imperceptibly led my heart to the peaceful emotion of friendship, and this emotion, together with the love of learning, made me tolerably happy.

These are not the idle musings of a sensitive soul, but a faithful account of something experienced. The truth is that Voltaire abandoned the marquise, not she him. She was merely mistaken about the details. It was not age and illness, or even satiety, which lessened Voltaire's desire for Mme Du Châtelet: he had simply fallen in love with another woman, and the other woman was his niece Mme Denis. An unpublished correspondence between uncle and niece has come to light. It contains full proof of my assertion, and has recently been published.[1] This correspondence also proves that in truth Voltaire sacrificed his happiness, if not his life, to his great affection for Mme Du Châtelet.

So when the marquise became Saint-Lambert's lover, she was not betraying Voltaire. But did she already love the young poet when she wrote the lines just quoted? We might think so, if in the same essay we did not hear this even more pathetic note: 'After we are thirty, passion does not carry us away with

---

[1] *Lettres d'amour de Voltaire à sa nièce* (Paris 1957); translated as *The Love Letters of Voltaire to his Niece* (London 1958).

the same impetuosity. I am sure that one could resist desire if
one tried very hard. . . .'

## VIII

Mme Du Châtelet died at Lunéville on 10 September 1749, and
was buried on the 11th in the vault of the canons (Archives of
Lunéville, GG 2, 39), in the church of Saint-Jacques, under the
centre aisle. Her tomb is covered by a slab of black marble,
without inscription.

# Le Vrai Voltaire par ses Lettres[1]

*à Jean Pommier*

Un mot d'explication et même d'excuse tout d'abord. Je crains
que vous ne trouviez le ton de ces conférences par trop personnel. Vous voyez que déjà j'ai prononcé un 'je', sinon deux.
Mais que voulez-vous? Depuis quarante ans je suis un fervent
de Voltaire (je me hâte d'ajouter que j'ai commencé fort
jeune — c'est à l'âge de dix ans que j'ai acheté ma première édition voltairienne), depuis vingt ans je passe tous mes jours en
sa compagnie, depuis six ans j'habite sa maison, je couche dans
sa chambre, dans sa bibliothèque je lis ses lettres, j'ouvre son
courrier, j'explore ses secrets les plus intimes; je suis devenu
un peu, *longo intervallo*, lui. Dans ces conditions ce ne serait
qu'hypocrisie ou affectation de vous parler du grand homme
sur un ton distant et impersonnel. Tout cela vous l'aurez compris, je le sais, et si je le souligne, c'est que j'ai tout de même
un immense avantage sur Voltaire: lui, il n'a jamais été invité
au Collège de France. Je ne voudrais pour rien au monde que
vous puissiez me croire capable d'abuser de cet honneur pour
faire de l'égotisme. Si je parle de Voltaire comme s'il était un
ami intime, c'est tout simplement qu'il l'est.

Il n'est pas facile non plus de comprimer dans les limites
de deux conférences tout ce que j'aurais voulu dire. J'ai été
obligé d'en faire plutôt un seul discours divisé arbitrairement
en deux parties, d'adopter un plan fort serré, avec des transitions quelque peu brusques. Permettez donc que je vous
présente une brève analyse de ce que vous allez entendre.

[1] Deux conférences faites au Collège de France, les 23 et 25 février 1959.
C'est avec grand plaisir que je remercie Madame la Princesse Del Drago de
m'avoir permis de donner devant un auditoire critique une lecture préalable
de ces conférences.

Je commence par quelques mots très généraux sur Voltaire;
suivent quelques considérations sur l'art et l'histoire du genre
épistolaire; nous verrons ensuite comme notre grand homme
se situe dans ce cadre, et le rôle unique de sa correspondance,
dont j'indique ensuite très brièvement l'étendue, la dispersion
et les avatars; à ceci s'ajoutent quelques mots sur les nouveaux
apports de mon édition; et enfin nous nous pencherons sur
une seule journée du grand homme; ce dernier chapitre, au
cours duquel j'aurai l'honneur de vous présenter des lettres
inédites assez remarquables, occupe la plus grande place dans
la deuxième partie de mon discours.

I

Presque deux siècles après sa mort, Voltaire est aussi vivant
que jamais: adoré par les uns, honni par les autres, mais s'impo-
sant à tous, émerveillant même ceux qui le détestent. Le nom
de Voltaire provoque toujours une réaction dans n'importe
quelle société et dans presque tous les pays — une réaction
plus ou moins favorable, plus ou moins informée, mais toujours témoin d'une influence vivante. Cette année 1959, qui
voit le bicentenaire de *Candide*, verra aussi la publication (à
ma connaissance) d'une trentaine de volumes consacrés à son
auteur; et les demandes de renseignements qui me parviennent
à cette occasion émanent de tous les continents. Tout le monde
est d'accord que *Candide* et les autres contes sont des chefs-
d'œuvre, et on n'a encore oublié ni le *Dictionnaire philosophique*,
ni cette extraordinaire histoire universelle qu'on ne peut com-
parer qu'à un vol d'aigle, ni le monument que Voltaire a érigé
à la gloire d'un siècle, ni tant d'autres écrits en tous genres et
sur tous les sujets. Pourtant, il n'y a qu'une partie de son œuvre
si immense et si variée que tous admirent sans réserve, et cette
partie, par une ironie du sort, n'est qu'un sous-produit de la
verve intarissable du philosophe, *parergon* que du reste il avait
horreur de voir imprimer. Qu'aurait-il dit s'il avait jamais
soupçonné qu'un jour on se mettrait à la publication de
ses moindres billets, de ses lettres les plus intimes? —

car, vous l'avez deviné, ce sous-produit, c'est en effet sa correspondance—il est certain que ce jour-là son courrier aurait été
enrichi de quelques vifs éclats de fureur et d'indignation.

En effet, Voltaire n'a pas hésité à qualifier certaine publication de ses lettres comme une offense au public et une violation
de tous les droits de la société; je n'ose presque pas ajouter
qu'il a également jugé digne du carcan les notes de l'éditeur.
Mais Scaliger, quoiqu'il ait qualifié l'éminent bibliographe
François Grudé de La Croix Du Maine de fou parce qu'il
'avoit une chambre toute pleine de lettres de divers personnages
mises dans des armoires, in nidis', a été obligé d'ajouter: 'Telles
gens sont les crocheteurs des hommes doctes, qui nous amas-
sent tout; cela nous sert beaucoup; il faut qu'il y ait de telles
gens.' En effet, la recherche de la vérité est sa propre justification: le rédacteur rougit, accepte avec fierté le titre de 'croche-
teur des hommes doctes', prend son courage à deux mains, et
continue.

II

Le néoplatonicien Proclus, dans son savant ouvrage περὶ ἐπι-
στολιμαίου χαρακτῆρος, a établi quarante et une catégories
de lettres. L'effort était méritoire, mais enfin la civilisation, on
nous le dit tous les jours, a fait d'immenses progrès depuis l'âge
de l'innocence. Et vraiment on se trouverait un peu à l'étroit
aujourd'hui avec un si petit nombre de cases. Où faudrait-il
consigner, par exemple, certaines lettres pastorales, ou les
épîtres comminatoires de tel homme d'état, ou le *fan-mail*
de Brigitte Bardot? Et puis, une catégorie telle que les lettres
d'amour par exemple ne présente en réalité qu'une homogé-
néité fort métaphysique. Autant de genres d'amour, autant de
genres de lettres. Nous avons de quoi construire un ample
système de classification décimale ou même duodécimale. Et
certainement ce n'est pas la difficulté de la chose qui me fait
renoncer à une structure plus scientifiquement détaillée et
nuancée que celle du grammairien constantinopolitain, pour
vous proposer plutôt une rigoureuse simplification. La raison

en est tout autre. En vérité, quand je regarde le vaste fleuve de lettres qui coule sans interruption depuis l'invention de l'écriture jusqu'à nous, je renonce à toute classification méthodique, car je m'aperçois que seules existent pour moi deux catégories de lettres : celles de Voltaire, et les autres. Eh oui, en s'occupant de cet être prestigieux on se voit entraîné malgré soi à cette sorte de constatations, qui ont tout l'air de rodomontades — et qui ne le sont pourtant pas, par le simple fait d'être vraies.

### III

Cicéron, Erasme, Madame de Sévigné, Horace Walpole, Voltaire, Bernard Shaw : ce sont les grands noms du genre épistolaire, et leur seule énumération suffit pour faire voir à quel point Voltaire est hors concours. Cicéron approche l'élégance du style voltairien, mais le nombre relativement petit de lettres que nous connaissons de lui reflète bien mal l'universalité de l'orateur. Erasme peint dans ses lettres toute une époque, mais ses correspondants sont peu nombreux, ses lettres rédigées dans une langue presque barbare, accessible aux seuls latinistes, et encore… On peut aimer à la folie toute la grâce, tout le charme, tout ce qu'il y a de vraiment *littéraire* dans les lettres de Madame de Sévigné, sans se faire d'illusions sur l'étroitesse de ses connaissances et de ses préoccupations. Quant à Horace Walpole, c'est un tout petit grand homme : jamais personne n'a plus longuement et profondément exploré la surface des choses. Heureusement aucun jugement de l'art épistolaire de Bernard Shaw n'est encore possible, puisque ses lettres ne sont connues que par bribes — quel trésor déjà ! Mais combien Voltaire est-il tout de même supérieur à Cicéron par son style, à Erasme par l'étendue sinon la profondeur de ses connaissances, à Madame de Sévigné par la grâce et les amitiés, à Walpole par l'universalité de ses intérêts et le nombre et la variété de ses correspondants !

### IV

Quelques mois avant sa mort, un journaliste interrogea Renan (oui, Renan, dont il est peut-être indiscret de prononcer le nom dans cette maison), il interrogea donc le vieux Renan sur l'évolution littéraire, et reçut une réponse qui avait de quoi surprendre l'enquêteur: 'Les modes littéraires . . .', dit-il, 'c'est puéril, c'est enfantin. Ce n'est pas intéressant, non, vraiment. . . .' Et il ajouta: 'La littérature elle-même, voyez-vous, c'est une préoccupation médiocre. . . .' Puis, se ravisant, il s'écria: 'Pardon, pardon, je retire ce que je viens de dire là, c'est exagéré. Racine a fait de bien belles choses, et Voltaire! Oh! les lettres de Voltaire, voyez-vous, c'est divin, quels trésors n'y a-t-il pas là-dedans! C'est admirable. . . .'[1]

En fait, il ne peut y avoir aucun doute que les lettres de Voltaire constituent le plus grand de tous les *biblia abiblia*, de la littérature malgré elle. Il existe à cela plusieurs raisons. Hormis une lettre d'enfant signée Zozo, les plus anciennes épîtres de Voltaire qui survivent datent de 1711, quand il était écolier. Il restait alors à Louis XIV quatre sombres années de déclin qui devaient être suivies de la trop brève régence du Duc d'Orléans et de l'interminable règne de Louis XV, bien-aimé de nom seulement; et Voltaire avait encore quelques années très actives devant lui quand Louis XVI monta sur le trône. Bref, il est né à l'apogée de l'ancien régime et ne mourut qu'une dizaine d'années avant la Révolution française. Sa correspondance englobe donc largement soixante années vitales, années durant lesquelles le monde moderne fut engendré.

Cela, certes, ne situe pas toute son histoire dans le temps. Les dons et la personnalité si brillants de Voltaire séduisirent des gens bien plus âgés que lui. Petit garçon il impressionna si fort Ninon de Lenclos (née en 1615, quatre-vingts ans avant lui) qu'elle le coucha, non pas comme on le répète trop souvent, dans son lit, mais sur son testament. Encore à l'école, il était traité en égal par Chaulieu, le dernier des poètes 'libertins', son aîné de soixante ans. On possède quelques-unes des délicieuses lettres, en prose et en vers, qu'ils s'écrivaient. A travers

---

[1] Jules Huret, *Enquête sur l'évolution littéraire* (Paris 1891), pp. 420–1; je dois cette citation à M. Henri Guillemin.

un Chaulieu, un Caumartin, un Prince de Vendôme, le jeune garçon braqua ses antennes loin à l'intérieur du grand siècle.

Et en 1718 le succès sans précédent de sa première pièce, *Œdipe*, fit de Voltaire, à l'âge de vingt-quatre ans, après dix-huit mois de prison et d'exil, avec tout ce que cela implique de conséquences et de symboles, le chef reconnu de la littérature française. Déjà les gens conservaient, achetaient, volaient, se passaient ses lettres, oui, et même les imprimaient. Adolescent, il eut une amourette avec une jeune fille dont la mère, journaliste de bas étage, s'empressa de publier les lettres qu'il écrivait à sa fille. Quelle mortification! Rien d'étonnant à ce qu'il ait toujours détesté voir publier ses lettres! On s'étonne même qu'il eût jamais pu en écrire une autre après cela.

v

Les publications de Voltaire étincelaient si visiblement de génie même quand il s'occupait des sujets les plus rébarbatifs, que sa réputation était extraordinairement étendue dans son propre pays et au-delà. Bien qu'avant tout créateur, Voltaire fut encore beaucoup plus: un historien original, un vulgarisateur scientifique, un réformateur social, un adversaire de toute religion en tant que superstition, un militant de la liberté et de la tolérance. C'est ce qui donne à ses œuvres et plus encore à sa correspondance une envergure aussi remarquable sous le rapport du contenu que sous celui de la durée. Et ceci se reflète dans l'étonnante qualité, variété et quantité de ses correspondants. En premier lieu ce sont naturellement ses semblables: Fontenelle, Alembert, Diderot, Helvétius, Vauvenargues, Rousseau, Buffon, Condorcet, Beaumarchais, Pope, Swift, même Lessing, ainsi que des personnages mineurs, en comparaison du moins avec les géants: Algarotti, Goldoni, Maffei et Spallanzani; Bernouilli et Haller; George Keate, Boswell et Horace Walpole; Sumarokov; Mayáns y Siscar; Jean Baptiste Rousseau, Maupertuis, Destouches, La Condamine, Moncrif, Voisenon, Prévost d'Exiles, Tressan, Piron, Mairan, Saurin,

Marmontel, Delisle de Salles, Mme de Graffigny, La Harpe, Du
Pont de Nemours, Mme d'Epinay, Mme Du Deffand, Ximenès,
Suard, Sedaine, Palissot, Chamfort, Mme Du Bocage, Florian,
Duclos, Dorat.

Je ne veux pas trop insister sur cet aspect de la correspondance, mais je ne peux pas m'empêcher de souligner un petit
détail qui ressort de cette énumération: Fontenelle est né en
1657, Suard et Du Pont de Nemours sont morts 160 ans plus
tard, en 1817. Il y a mieux: en 1769, Voltaire écrit au Duc
d'Aumont (dans une lettre inédite): 'Mon premier protecteur
fut votre bisayeul' — or, ce bisaïeul était né en 1632, ce qui
représente un pont de 185 ans.

Voltaire correspondait aussi avec bon nombre des principaux
hommes d'état de l'Europe, depuis Dubois, Fleury, les Argenson, Amelot, Bernis, Maurepas, Richelieu, Choiseul et Turgot,
jusqu'à Bolingbroke et Wilkes; l'Autrichien Kaunitz; le Suédois
Bernstorff; les Allemands Podewils et Cocceji; le Suisse François Tronchin; le Hongrois Fekete de Galánta; l'Espagnol
Miranda; les Russes Chouvaloff, Vorontsoff et Golitzine.

Il fut en relations amicales, et même intimes dans certains
cas, avec beaucoup des grandes dames du siècle, y compris la
Marquise de Bernières, les Duchesses d'Aiguillon, Mme Du-
pin, la Duchesse Du Maine, la Marquise de Pompadour, la
Duchesse de Choiseul, Mme Necker, Mme de Saint-Julien,
la Comtesse Bentinck, et par-dessus tout avec la savante, la
scintillante, la bien-aimée Emilie Du Châtelet, dont je viens
d'avoir l'honneur de publier la correspondance.

Pour ce qui est des têtes couronnées à qui il écrivait d'égal à
égal quoiqu'à l'époque ils participaient encore de la divinité qui
entourait le trône, Voltaire était le correspondant préféré de
deux des plus remarquables monarques de tous les temps, Frédéric II, roi de Prusse, et Catherine II, Impératrice de toutes les
Russies: Frédéric, son disciple, son cher ami, ou plutôt son
ennemi bien-aimé; Catherine, peut-être parce qu'ils ne se ren-
contrèrent jamais, tout simplement son disciple. Une liste complète des autres princes régnants correspondants de Voltaire

serait fastidieuse: je ne mentionnerai, à côté des rois d'Angle-
terre et de France, et les reines de Prusse, qu'Ulrica de Suède;
Christian VII de Danemark; Wilhelmine, Margrave de Bay-
reuth; Charles Théodore, Électeur Palatin; Louise Dorothée,
Duchesse de Saxe-Gotha; Caroline Louise, Margrave de Baden-
Durlach; le Prince de Ligne; Stanislas Leszczynsky et Stanislas
Poniatowsky, Rois de Pologne; Charles Eugène et Louis
Eugène, Ducs de Wurtemberg; et beaucoup d'autres, de même
que des princes de l'église comme les papes Benoît XIV et
Clément XIII, et de nombreux cardinaux et évêques, y compris
Tencin, Passionei et Quirini, en laissant de côté des person-
nages aussi exotiques que, par exemple, Gabriel Podosky,
Prince-Archevêque de Pologne et de Lituanie, et Biord, Prince-
Archevêque de Genève.

Ces énumérations sont loin de couvrir l'étendue de la correspondance de Voltaire — bien sûr, puisqu'il a eu 1 200 correspondants. Je n'ai rien dit des lettres, dont certaines sont parmi
les plus passionnantes, à des acteurs et actrices; ni de celles à
des artistes, médecins, éditeurs, financiers, banquiers; ni celles
aux nombreuses académies dont il était membre dans plusieurs
pays; je n'ai rien dit de ses lettres à sa famille; et je ne puis faire
qu'une brève allusion à la longue et profondément intéressante
série de lettres à des amis de jeunesse, amis de toujours: Argental, Cideville, Thieriot. Et il y a ici une constatation fort remarquable à faire, constatation qui devrait en elle-même suffire
à prouver la fausseté de l'image que tant de gens se font d'un
Voltaire frondeur et invivable. Je viens de prononcer les noms
de trois amis seulement: mais voici ce qui est impressionnant,
c'est que dans la liste de ses correspondants on trouve environ
trente-cinq noms de personnes avec qui Voltaire a entretenu
une correspondance suivie pendant vingt ans, et une vingtaine
de correspondances ininterrompues, en dehors de sa famille,
qui ont duré au-delà de trente ans. Qui parmi nous pourrait en
dire autant — même ceux qui ont dépassé leurs quatre-vingts
ans comme Voltaire?

Notons en passant que la correspondance de Voltaire, bien

qu'écrite naturellement pour la plus grande part en français,
comprend aussi pas mal de lettres en anglais et en italien, et on
y trouve même du latin, de l'allemand et de l'espagnol.

## VI

Tout ceci est peu banal, en fait cela est sans parallèle. Une correspondance d'une telle durée et d'un si vaste intérêt serait de
toute façon historiquement importante, sans devoir être pour
autant de la littérature. C'est pourtant là le caractère unique des
lettres de Voltaire. Ce qui fait d'un simple document un mor-
ceau de littérature, c'est la personnalité de l'auteur, la qualité de
ce qu'il exprime et la manière dont il l'exprime. Il y a là une
nuance sensible. Il y a ceux qui écrivent en général bien, et
même superlativement, et qui sont incapables d'écrire une
bonne lettre. La correspondance de Baudelaire en est la preuve
parmi tant d'autres. En revanche, il y a ceux qui écrivent de
très bonnes lettres tout en étant parfaitement incapables de
faire, par exemple, un roman ou un conte, qui ne paraissent
pourtant que le développement d'une lettre; nous en connaissons tous des exemples parmi nos relations. Il n'est pas question
ici de style. Même les écrivains dont le style est extrêmement
artificiel — tels Henry James, Proust, James Joyce — ont
écrit d'admirables lettres, de même que certains — tel Flaubert — qui se sont donné énormément de peine pour par-
venir à des effets simples et coulants. Je crois que l'essentiel
est plutôt psychologique. L'écrivain écrit pour le public — que
ce public soit même très limité est indifférent; l'épistolier écrit
à quelqu'un en particulier.

On voit sans autre que ceci fait appel à des qualités très pré-
cises, dont certaines peut-être inattendues. L'essentiel est évidemment la capacité de se mettre en rapport avec la personne
à qui l'on s'adresse. Voltaire avait ce don à un degré presque
miraculeux. Le voir décrire le même événement, faire la même
réflexion à un ancien ami, à un confrère d'académie, à une
femme, à un jeune protégé, à un voisin de campagne, est toute

une éducation. Non pas qu'il cherche nécessairement à plaire —
innombrables sont les lettres qui sont très loin d'une telle
préoccupation — mais de toucher, d'intéresser chacun par
l'aspect de la chose qui correspond à ses propres intérêts, ten-
dances, croyances. 'Accusez moi si vous voulez d'un Excès de
vanité,' lui dit un jour Mme Du Deffand (1 mars 1769), 'mais
vous ne dites rien que Je ne crois avoir pensé.' Pourrait-on
mieux définir une bonne lettre? Et Voltaire a répondu (15 mars
1769): 'On se met sans peine au ton de ceux à qui on parle; il
n'en est pas de même quand on écrit; c'est un hasard si l'on
rencontre juste.' Un hasard! étrange hasard qui favorisait Voltaire chaque fois qu'il prenait plume en main!

Il faut également beaucoup de générosité d'esprit, et de générosité tout court, pour qu'un grand homme écrive de bonnes
lettres. Songez que Bernard Shaw touchait des cachets astrono-
miques pour tout ce qu'il publiait, et que sa moindre lettre était
devenue une marchandise précieuse — cela ne l'empêchait pas
de répondre très souvent et très longuement à de jeunes écrivains et de jeunes acteurs qui sollicitaient ses conseils et son
appui. Ce n'était pas exactement le cas de Voltaire, puisqu'il
ne touchait jamais un sou de ses écrits; mais songez aux occu-
pations de cet homme, seigneur de village, justicier de haute et
basse justice, cultivateur, bâtisseur, homme d'affaires, chef de
famille, et même, à ses moments perdus, auteur de quelques milliers d'écrits sous 150 pseudonymes. Tout cela ne l'empêchait
point d'écrire des lettres à un Helvétius ou à un Chabanon
commentant longuement leurs écrits; à un Damilaville ou un
Argence pour les encourager à écraser l'infâme; à Mme Du
Deffand pour la consoler de sa méchanceté et de sa cécité; à
Frédéric pour le détourner du suicide; à Catherine pour l'encourager à libérer les serfs ou à écraser Moustapha; à tout le
monde pour solliciter des souscriptions pour Mlle Corneille,
pour agiter l'opinion publique en faveur de Calas, de Sirven et
de tant d'autres; à ses banquiers, ses hommes d'affaires pour
des questions d'argent; à ses éditeurs et imprimeurs pour se
plaindre de leur travail, de leurs lenteurs, des coquilles, des

mauvais caractères employés, des trop grandes ou trop petites marges; d'innombrables lettres de simple amitié, voisinage ou consolation.

Il est de rigueur aujourd'hui de dire que l'art épistolaire est tout simplement fonction de la distance, qu'on n'écrit pas ce qu'on peut dire, que la rapidité des communications, et avant tout le téléphone, nous permettent de tout dire, et que par conséquent l'art de la lettre est mort. Il me semble parfaitement évident que ce lieu commun, comme tant d'autres, est faux. J'ai déjà cité Bernard Shaw; on pourrait ajouter de nombreux autres cas. Et les lettres de Proust? et la correspondance Gide–Claudel? et les lettres de D. H. Lawrence? et ce volume extraordinaire qui vient de paraître avec un choix des éruptions épistolaires de Thomas Wolfe? Il n'est même pas vrai qu'on écrive moins — nous le verrons dans un instant. Tout ce qui est vrai, c'est que certains genres très limités de lettres ne s'écrivent plus, ou beaucoup moins. Une très grande partie des charmants billets de Voltaire à son éditeur genevois aurait certainement été remplacée par de très fréquents coups de téléphone. Cela aurait été bien dommage, mais enfin cela justifie assez peu le pessimisme total affecté par les historiens et les anthologistes.

Il est vrai qu'autrefois l'arrivée et le départ du courrier était un grand événement; on se préparait à envoyer et à recevoir les lettres; on se donnait par conséquent quelque peine pour les écrire, d'autant plus que c'était normalement le destinataire qui payait le port, souvent fort élevé. Mais ce que les lettres ont perdu dans ce sens ne l'ont-elles peut-être pas gagné en naturel? Hélas, les transformations de la vie sociale et familiale ont produit aussi un résultat contraire: la peur de se laisser aller. Nombreux sont ceux de nos jours qui sont hantés, même en écrivant les lettres les plus intimes, par la crainte de les entendre un jour citées au cours d'un procès. Passons.

Du reste, il ne faut pas s'imaginer que l'absence du téléphone et la difficulté des voyages amenèrent automatiquement la production de bonnes lettres. En réalité, même au dix-huitième

siècle français, cette fine fleur de la civilisation courtoise, il n'y
a guère, il faut le reconnaître franchement, que Jean Jacques
Rousseau, Diderot, Frédéric II, Mme Du Deffand, Mlle de
Lespinasse, Mme Du Châtelet, Catherine II, dont quelques
lettres soient entrées dans la littérature française à côté de la
masse immense de celles de Voltaire — et il n'est pas indifférent de noter que cette courte liste comprend les noms d'un
Suisse, d'un Prussien et d'une Russe née allemande. C'est là
précisément le miracle Voltaire, que parmi tant de lettres, il
faille chercher longuement pour en trouver d'ennuyeuses.

## VII

Car enfin, quoique à la rigueur une lettre puisse être intéressante
même mal écrite, elle ne résistera cependant pas à l'usure du
temps : *a fortiori* une correspondance de vingt, cent, cinq cents,
voire vingt mille lettres. Pour survivre, c'est-à-dire pour devenir de la littérature, il faut tout de même qu'une lettre ait des
qualités littéraires. Et c'est là bien sûr que triomphe Voltaire.
Il avait un sens instinctif du mot et de la phrase, sens à tel point
affiné par une discipline incessante, qu'il lui était impossible
d'écrire une ligne banale ou d'en dicter une — car il écrivait
comme il parlait et parlait comme il écrivait : nulle différence,
ou à peine, entre une lettre dictée et une lettre écrite de sa main.
Peu de différence également entre les lettres du jeune homme
et du vieillard. Les premières sont peut-être plus poétiques,
mais en général c'est le même vocabulaire, toujours enrichi avec
le temps, mais restant dans le même genre, vocabulaire où les
échos du latin de Louis-le-grand, les lectures des anciens poètes
français et des penseurs anglais modernes, viennent si heureusement se mélanger aux expressions techniques de la jurispru-
dence et des arts et métiers, aux parlers de la Bourgogne et de
Genève ; partout l'on retrouve la même grâce coulante, la même
passion, la même sincérité, le même sérieux, la même sensibilité
raisonnante, la même spontanéité, le même amour de l'anti-
thèse, le même esprit, bref, le même style. Ses moindres notes

d'affaires, même les plus ordinaires, évoquent toujours un sourire ou une grimace sympathique.

Et quel cours de style épistolaire! Comment se plaindre à son éditeur de n'avoir pas reçu d'épreuves ce jour-là: 'Je suis tout stupéfait de ne rien recevoir de cher Gabriel. Je ne suis point accoutumé à un tel oubli. Un jour sans feuille est un jour perdu et ce n'était pas la peine de venir se faire chamois des Alpes pour éprouver de tels revers. A quoi donc sacrifiez-vous Jeanne, l'Histoire, Oreste? Cela me tue.' (Soit dit en passant, cette expression 'un jour perdu' est l'une des allusions classiques favorites de Voltaire: selon Suétone, l'empereur Titus ayant laissé passer un jour sans faire de présent s'exclama: 'Amici, diem perdidi.')

Comment se défendre d'un faux: 'J'ai vu', écrit-il au Duc de Grafton, 'J'ai vu dans le *Whitehall Evening-Post*, du 7 octobre 1769, no. 3668, une prétendue lettre de moi à sa majesté le roi de Prusse: cette lettre est bien sotte; cependant je ne l'ai point écrite.' Et il signe.

Comment consulter son médecin:

Un vieillard de soixante et seize ans est attaqué depuis longtemps d'une humeur scorbutique qui l'a toujours réduit à une très grande maigreur, qui lui a enlevé presque toutes ses dents, qui s'attache quelque fois aux amygdales, qui lui cause souvent des borborygmes, des insomnies &c. &c. attachées à cette maladie, supplie M. Bouvard de vouloir bien avoir la bonté d'écrire au bas de ce billet s'il pense que le lait de chèvre pourrait procurer quelques soulagements. Il est ridicule peut-être de prétendre guérir à cet âge; mais le malade ayant quelques affaires qui ne pourront être finies que dans six mois, il prend la liberté de demander si le lait de chèvre pourrait le mener jusques là? Il demande si on a l'expérience que le lait de chèvre, avec quelques purgations absolument nécessaires, ait fait quelque bien en cas pareil?

Enfin, car je ne peux évidemment vous citer que quelques exemples et de très courts, enfin, dans un autre ordre d'idées, c'est en ces termes que Voltaire, à l'âge de quatre-vingt-quatre ans, peu de jours avant sa mort, refusait l'invitation d'une dame sur un petit chiffon de papier que possède l'Institut et Musée Voltaire: 'Je sais bien ce que je désire, mais je ne sais pas ce que je ferai. Je suis malade, je souffre de la tête aux pieds. Il n'y a que mon cœur de sain, et cela n'est bon à rien.'

Et en plus de tout cela, les lettres de Voltaire contiennent quelques-uns de ses vers de circonstance les plus charmants, avec ici et là une touche plus profonde de poésie.

Il est vrai que les circonstances tout à fait spéciales de la vie de Voltaire ont beaucoup contribué à faire de lui un grand épistolier. Sa vie dans ce sens se divise en trois parties assez nettement définies. Il y a d'abord l'époque mondaine. Voltaire habite Paris et de là visite ses amis jusqu'à Forges et La Rivière Bourdet au nord; Caen vers l'ouest; Richelieu, Ussé, La Source et Sully plus au sud; sans parler des maisons autour de Paris, Sceaux, Maisons, Vaux, et tant d'autres. Cette période pourrait s'appeler celle des lettres de château, c'est l'époque où se trouvent les belles lettres en prose et en vers adressées aux Chaulieu, Ussé, Brancas, Sully et tant d'autres.

Ensuite c'est l'époque de l'absence de la capitale, du séjour en Angleterre, puis à Cirey, aux Pays-Bas, en Prusse; ici se situent les grandes lettres philosophiques et scientifiques, adressées à Frédéric, à Maupertuis, à Mairan, et cent autres; c'est l'époque des lettres de réflexion.

Enfin, c'est la période d'exil. Voltaire est entièrement absent de Paris pendant un quart de siècle, et c'est la période de la correspondance massive, avec le monde entier, puisque les lettres sont devenues presque le seul moyen de communication avec le monde extérieur. Il devient en tout premier lieu le philosophe. C'est l'époque des lettres de propagande et d'action.

Il est évident que si Voltaire était resté tranquillement chez lui, sa correspondance aurait été très différente, beaucoup plus limitée, et infiniment moins intéressante.

## VIII

Permettez ici un petit mot d'avertissement. Juger la valeur profonde d'une lettre de Voltaire est une tâche des plus nuancées.

Parmi ces lettres il y en a dans toutes les manières : la seule liste des correspondants en est la preuve. Dans ces conditions il est évident que toutes les lettres n'expriment pas également les vraies pensées et sentiments de celui qui les écrit. L'épanchement tout entier d'une lettre adressée à un ami intime dans un moment de douleur ou de joie trahit l'écrivain avec une vérité évidente : mais ce que Voltaire ressent souvent varie et même très rapidement. Il y a là en effet une vérité peut-être profonde, mais qui risque de n'être que passagère.

Une lettre destinée par contre à être lue par d'autres que son destinataire, et même à être imprimée, pourrait à première vue exiger une lecture prudente. Mais cela n'est pas invariable, puisque dans une telle lettre Voltaire souvent se donne beaucoup de peine pour exprimer avec clarté ses vraies pensées sur tel ou tel sujet. Même là il y a des nuances. Voltaire n'ignorait pas que certains de ses correspondants, Mme Du Deffand par exemple, malgré leurs protestations, faisait lire ses lettres devant les fidèles de leurs salons. Là, Voltaire écrivait des lettres intimes, mais pourtant exprimées de telle façon qu'elles pouvaient être vues par d'autres yeux que ceux de l'intéressé. Problème délicat, et les brouillons de ses lettres à Mme Du Deffand témoignent des peines que Voltaire s'est données pour le résoudre.

Et puis, dans les lettres les plus intimes, écrites à un Argental, un Thieriot, un Damilaville, qui communiquaient avec lui par une espèce de langue secrète, Voltaire très souvent disait le contraire du sens littéral de ses propres paroles. Une fois ce petit langage appris (il n'est pas question ici des lettres plus ou moins chiffrées, pour lesquelles il y a une clef à débrouiller) on parvient sans difficulté à distinguer les formules par lesquelles Voltaire désavoue certains ouvrages, celles qui indiquent à ses amis parisiens que tel ouvrage n'était vraiment pas de lui, ou était de lui mais ne devait absolument pas être avoué, ou était de lui et pouvait être avoué tacitement, ou était de lui et devait être attribué à un autre, et ainsi de suite avec des variantes presque infinies. On devine combien d'erreurs ont été commises par des commentateurs ignorant ces petits mystères.

L'erreur est souvent faite d'attribuer aux écrivains les sentiments qu'ils mettent dans la bouche des personnages qu'ils ont
créés: l'erreur est vulgaire et reconnue comme telle. Mais celui
qui cite les lettres de Voltaire sans tenir compte des difficultés
souvent fort subtiles que je ne viens de brosser que fort légèrement, serait coupable d'une erreur presque aussi grave. Le plus
innombrable personnage créé par Voltaire, c'est Voltaire lui-
même, il agite ce personnage comme une marionnette, on ne
l'enferme pas dans une camisole de force.

## IX

Combien Voltaire écrivit-il de lettres? Eh bien, mes classeurs,
mes fichiers, mes listes chronologiques et alphabétiques signa-
lent la présence de vingt mille lettres, dont neuf sur dix soit en
manuscrit, soit en photocopie — à peu près un quart de million
de feuilles de papier en tout — car je possède beaucoup de lettres
dans plusieurs, voire jusqu'à dix, douze et même quinze textes:
brouillons, originaux, copies destinées aux archives de Voltaire,
transcriptions contemporaines, éditions avec variantes, variantes souvent imaginées par Voltaire lui-même dans les lettres
qu'il a livrées à l'impression — mais c'étaient là des lettres
ostensibles ou d'apparat — jamais il n'a imprimé une lettre
personnelle. Certaines périodes de sa vie nous fournissent un
grand nombre de lettres; mais ces époques sont rares et courtes.
Pour d'autres périodes, tout spécialement au début, nous en
avons relativement peu, pour d'autres encore, comme lorsque
Voltaire poursuivait activement un but particulier, nous en
avons beaucoup, mais nous savons qu'il en écrivit plus encore.
Ainsi, en octobre 1748, Voltaire fit de grands efforts pour empêcher que soit représentée une parodie de sa tragédie *Sémiramis*. Nous avons les lettres qu'il écrivit à ce propos le 10 à la
reine de France, au chef de la police et à l'*ange* d'Argental; mais
il nous dit lui-même — non pas vaguement qu'il a écrit encore
trente lettres, remarque purement symbolique mille fois citée
comme si elle avait une valeur statistique — il nous dit très

précisément qu'il a écrit aussi à Mme de Pompadour, à la Duchesse d'Aiguillon, à Maurepas, au Duc d'Aumont, à la Duchesse de Villars, au Duc de Fleury et au Duc de Gèvres — correspondance bien ducale ce jour-là : toutes ces lettres se sont perdues, ou du moins n'ont pas encore été retrouvées.

Est-il étonnant que celui qui plonge en profondeur dans cet océan a souvent le même sens de l'infini qu'a exprimé Newton en face de l'univers qu'il venait de dévoiler ? Ce sens est incommunicable, on ne peut que le symboliser par des chiffres, eux-mêmes à peine saisissables. L'astronome exprime sa stupeur en années-lumière ; heureusement nous n'en sommes pas là. Je vous demande pourtant la permission de vous présenter quelques statistiques tout aussi bouleversantes à l'échelle humaine. Mais il faut d'abord que je vous détrompe sur un détail. On dit très souvent que Voltaire a écrit énormément de lettres. Il n'en est rien. Faites le calcul. Je vous ai déjà dit que j'ai pu retrouver 20 000 lettres. Or laissant de côté une lettre d'enfance, la correspondance de Voltaire s'échelonne sur 67 années ; 67 années ont 3 484 semaines ; 3 484 semaines ont 24 388 jours — sans compter les années bissextiles. Nous arrivons donc à une moyenne d'à peine une lettre par jour. Je crois que nous possédons très approximativement une lettre sur deux de toutes celles que Voltaire a écrites. Dans ce cas la moyenne s'élève à deux par jour. C'est peu absolument, c'est même peu relativement. Car il semble, d'après les journaux américains, que l'ex-Président Hoover ait écrit au cours d'une seule année, et c'était sa quatre-vingt-quatrième, 55 952 lettres.[1] Ça, c'est beaucoup. C'est même incroyable, puisque cela fait une moyenne de 155 lettres par jour à condition que M. Hoover travaillât 365 jours par an. Mais même très fortement exagéré, ce chiffre fait pâlir les pauvres 20 000 lettres de toute la vie de Voltaire que je donne dans mon édition. En effet, ce qui est remarquable, ce n'est pas le nombre de lettres que Voltaire a écrites, mais le nombre de celles que ses correspondants ont tenu à garder depuis sa jeunesse. A part les archivistes par nécessité, et les collectionneurs par les pires

[1] *Time* (international edition), 18 August 1958, p. 31.

caractéristiques de ce genre de personnes, qui est-ce qui gardera jamais une lettre de M. Hoover, et combien en restera-t-il de vivantes après deux siècles dans ces mètres cubes qui font de nos jours la mesure des acquisitions archivales de tous les pays?

Je donne donc dans mon édition 20 000 lettres, le double de ce qui se trouve dans les éditions précédentes. Ces vingt mille lettres sont adressées à 1 200 correspondants, dont 400 nouveaux, et formeront 80 volumes, dont 39 déjà publiés, dans un texte commenté par environ 200 000 notes, et accompagné de quelque 250 appendices, et plusieurs centaines d'illustrations.

## x

Voltaire ayant écrit à tant de personnes dans tant de pays, et ses lettres ayant été si assidûment collectionnées pendant deux siècles et demi, il n'est pas surprenant qu'elles soient largement dispersées. Des manuscrits — car l'édition est naturellement basée sur les textes originaux — ont en effet été trouvés dans près de 300 collections publiques et privées un peu partout, de Tartu à Naples et de Honolulu à Wisbech. Parmi les collections qui possèdent des manuscrits voltairiens, la Gossoudarstvennaya biblioteka poublitchnaya imyeni Saltykoff-Chtchedrina à Leningrad doit rester en dehors de toute classification, *facile princeps*, puisqu'elle contient la bibliothèque de Voltaire,[1] y compris une grande partie de ses archives, sans parler des innombrables notes de sa main qui ornent les marges des imprimés. A part ce fonds merveilleux, la plus belle collection de manuscrits voltairiens, tenant compte en même temps de la qualité et de la quantité, si j'ose me permettre de le dire avec si peu de discrétion, est actuellement celle de l'Institut et Musée Voltaire, aux Délices de Voltaire; en deuxième place vient celle de la Bibliothèque nationale, qui est d'une remarquable richesse grâce surtout à Cayrol et à Seymour de Ricci;

---

[1] L'Institut et Musée Voltaire vient de publier le catalogue établi par Voltaire lui-même, et sous sa direction, de sa bibliothèque à Ferney: *Voltaire's Catalogue of his Library at Ferney*, edited by George R. Havens and Norman Torrey, *Studies on Voltaire and the Eighteenth Century* (Genève 1959), tome ix.

ensuite il y a la collection de la Pierpont Morgan Library à New York, composée en grande partie de pièces de la plus grande classe; et en quatrième place se trouve la collection particulière de la Reine des Pays-Bas, si gracieusement mise à ma disposition. Remarquables également sont les collections de la Bibliothèque historique de la ville de Paris, de la Bibliothèque royale de Belgique (grâce au Comte de Launoit), de la Bibliothèque publique et universitaire de Genève. A ma connaissance, il se trouve actuellement des manuscrits de la correspondance de Voltaire dans des collections de dix-neuf pays (quoique ma définition d'un pays soit peut-être trop large): Algérie, Allemagne, Autriche, Belgique, Canada, Danemark, Estonie, Etats-Unis, Finlande, Grande-Bretagne, Hawaï, Italie, Lithuanie, Pays-Bas, Pologne, Russie, Suède, Suisse. Quant à la France, j'y ai retrouvé des manuscrits dans soixante-sept archives, bibliothèques et collections privées.

Je tiens sans doute ici la meilleure occasion qui puisse jamais se présenter à moi de remercier les nombreux archivistes, bibliothécaires et particuliers, et les quelques libraires, qui m'ont si généreusement accordé leur aide et communiqué leurs trésors, sous forme de vente, de prêt ou de reproduction photographique. Je les en remercie de tout cœur publiquement; ils sont du reste tous nommés dans les notes de chaque lettre et dans la préface de chaque volume de mon édition. Ceci est également l'occasion pour moi de mettre au pilori le très petit nombre de ceux qui ont refusé leur concours. Ceux-là, je ne les ai pas encore nommés, je laisse subsister l'espoir, mais....

## XI

D'une façon ou d'une autre, ce qui survit de la correspondance de Voltaire est maintenant connu en manuscrit pour les neuf dixièmes. Ce chiffre serait encore plus élevé sans la disparition pendant et après la guerre de nombreux papiers de collections détruites ou pillées — bien que quelques-uns d'entre eux commencent à réapparaître. Par exemple, les lettres du Roi

Frédéric à Voltaire qui sont produites prudemment, petit à petit, sur le marché des autographes, ont été volées dans les archives prussiennes de Berlin. *Caveat emptor!*

L'examen d'originaux si nombreux (environ 250 000 pages manuscrites) a révélé entre autres choses l'état désespérément défectueux de la correspondance publiée. Déjà de son vivant, trente brochures et volumes furent consacrés exclusivement aux lettres de Voltaire, pour la plupart interceptées ou volées, si grande était la soif qu'en avait le public. Dans ces publications a commencé le processus de corruption. Juxtapositions judicieuses, sélections prudentes, une omission ou une adjonction ingénieuse ici et là, amusait fort la galerie, tandis que Voltaire, sans recours, enrageait. Ce dont on ne se rend pas compte, c'est que ce processus a toujours continué depuis. Beaumarchais et Condorcet, dans la grande et belle édition de Kehl, avaient à respecter les susceptibilités de nombreux correspondants, y compris Catherine et Frédéric, qui étaient toujours en vie. Il n'y avait jamais eu aucune édition séparée de la correspondance de Voltaire dans son ensemble, mais dans chaque édition successive de ses œuvres (il y en a eu plus de cinquante, allant de trois volumes en caractères microscopiques, jusqu'à 125 volumes) le texte des lettres a subi les divagations du goût et de la censure; et comme chaque éditeur modifiait ordinairement le texte sur la base de celui qui lui venait de son prédécesseur, tous ces changements se sont accumulés.

Certaines des ces altérations n'étaient qu'amusantes. Voici un cas, qui en même temps lève un peu le voile qui cache la personnalité d'Alembert. En effet, on ignore le vrai caractère du mathématicien-philosophe. C'est seulement quand on a pris connaissance des nombreux passages et des lettres entières jusqu'à présent supprimés, qu'on s'aperçoit à quel point il était tout de même mal embouché. Voici donc Alembert qui révèle à Voltaire l'auteur de la comédie des *Philosophes* dans laquelle Rousseau, Diderot et d'autres sont brutalement attaqués. Dans sa lettre Alembert appelle Palissot un 'maquereau', et il nomme plusieurs femmes distinguées comme étant ses protectrices, les décrivant comme des 'catins en fonctions et des putains honoraires'. L'édition de Kehl réduisit 'maquereau' à l'initiale, supprima les noms des dames, imprima 'catins', mais changea 'putains' en 'catins'. Un éditeur du début du dix-neuvième siècle, le bibliographe Renouard, qui pour une fois consulta le manuscrit, restaura 'maquereau' et les noms des dames, mais, avec une sollicitude prudemment discriminative, réduisit à la fois 'catins' et 'putains' aux initiales; toutefois, il ne le fit qu'en principe, car, ne pouvant donner à chaque terme son initiale propre, puisque celle de 'catin' eût suggéré un mot moins imprimable encore, il représenta l'un et l'autre par un 'p'. Voilà en miniature tout un cours de relativité morale, d'histoire des mœurs, et de transmission des textes.

Puisque je suis sur le chapitre d'Alembert, permettez que je vous cite un autre exemple le concernant, fort amusant en même temps qu'un peu sérieux. Ayant appris de Voltaire les événements funestes de Genève du 15 février 1770, Alembert répond, avec son insensibilité habituelle: 'On s'égorge donc dans Genève, dieu merci, et ce n'est pas pour la consubstantialité ou consubstantiabilité du verbe.' Remercier dieu qu'on s'égorge à Genève, cela était jugé un peu trop corsé pour les tendres susceptibilités des lecteurs de Voltaire. Et puis c'était si facile à corriger! on n'avait qu'à déplacer légèrement une toute petite conjonction, et le brave Alembert devint parfaitement respectable. Dans toutes les éditions, en effet, au lieu du 'On s'égorge donc dans Genève, dieu merci, et ce n'est pas pour' etc., on trouve: 'On s'égorge donc dans Genève, et dieu merci, ce n'est pas pour la consubstantialité ou consubstantiabilité.'

D'autres changements, pourtant, sont bien plus graves encore, tels des passages et même des lettres entières supprimés, transposés ou modifiés à les rendre méconnaissables, et les cas où deux, trois et même dix ou douze lettres furent mises en pièces et un choix des fragments rassemblés pour former des amalgames ahurissants. Tout cela peut être remis en ordre, non sans quelque peine il est vrai, chaque fois que les manuscrits originaux peuvent être retrouvés et collationnés. Mais il y a d'autres difficultés moins faciles à surmonter. Certaines d'entre elles sont dues à Voltaire lui-même. La pire, c'est la datation, qui est souvent de la plus haute importance du point de vue historique et biographique. Voltaire lui-même datait rarement une lettre complètement, souvent il ne mettait qu'un jour et un mois, tout aussi souvent un jour seulement et très souvent aussi, hélas, point de date du tout.

A ce sujet il se présente une difficulté souvent angoissante: c'est que beaucoup de lettres de Voltaire portent des dates ajoutées par d'autres mains, dates très souvent fausses. J'ai parlé dans la préface des *Lettres d'amour de Voltaire à sa nièce* d'un exemple bouleversant de cette difficulté. Sur les 142 lettres inédites publiées dans ce volume il n'y en a que trois qui sont complètement datées; sur la plus grande partie des autres Mme Denis elle-même a ajouté une date. Qui était mieux placé pour le faire? Hélas, ces dates sont fausses, non pas ici et là, mais le plus souvent. Plus la date qu'elle ajoute est précise, plus elle risque d'être erronée. C'est ainsi que nous avons une lettre qu'elle a datée du 2 septembre 1743, et une autre qui porte de sa main un 12 octobre 1745. Or, la lettre qui porte le 2 septembre 1743 est en réalité de février 1742, et celle datée du 12 octobre 1745 ne peut être que du 7 décembre 1747. Je connais même une autre lettre encore inédite (du 31 mai 1768) de Voltaire à sa nièce, où Mme Denis, en la datant, s'est trompée de trente ans.

Tout cela aidera peut-être à faire comprendre pourquoi quinze années de déblayage furent nécessaires avant que la publication de l'édition critique de la correspondance de Voltaire pût commencer, et pourquoi dix autres années auront encore passé avant que l'ouvrage soit achevé d'imprimer.

## XII

Pourquoi le texte des lettres de Voltaire est-il si incomplet et si défectueux? La réponse à cette question est de deux ordres

d'une importance pratique à peu près égale: le premier philosophique, le second technique. Voltaire a toujours tenu une
place tout à fait spéciale dans l'esprit des Français. Il était le
chef des philosophes, il était même *le* philosophe; ce fait, joint
à sa grandeur purement littéraire, a fait de lui en même temps
la cible de toutes les réactions et le triomphateur de toutes les
attaques. Dans le domaine littéraire on a de cette constatation
une preuve éclatante: c'est que le plus grand nombre d'éditions
des œuvres du grand classique a été publié précisément pendant
les années qui ont vu le triomphe du romantisme. Dans le
domaine de la sensibilité, la tendance même la plus accusée
ne devient que rarement exclusive. Mais ce genre de générosité
intellectuelle n'existe guère dans le domaine des croyances
religieuses et politiques. Et en effet le revirement malheureux
de tant de Français vers des opinions extrêmes dans les deux
sens a presque entièrement bloqué depuis de longues années
les études voltairiennes approfondies et de longue haleine.
Déjà, dès la fin de 1867, moment où un triste avenir se laissait
entrevoir, Flaubert s'exclamait dans une lettre (édition Conard,
v. 344): 'Si nous sommes tellement bas moralement et politi-
quement, c'est qu'au lieu de suivre la grande route de M. de
Voltaire, c'est à dire celle de la Justice et du Droit, on a pris
les sentiers de Rousseau, qui, par le sentiment, nous ont
ramenés au catholicisme. Si on avait eu souci de l'Equité et non
de la Fraternité, nous serions haut.' Pour donner toute sa valeur
à cette parole, il faut savoir ce que Flaubert entend par 'fraternité'; mais même sans le comprendre on reconnaît là les paroles
d'un homme qui a saisi ce que représente Voltaire dans notre
courant intellectuel. Je n'insiste pas. Il y a là, me semble-t-il,
une étude fort significative à faire: mais cette tâche, c'est à un
Français qu'elle incombe.

L'explication technique à laquelle j'ai fait allusion, de l'état
déplorable du texte des lettres de Voltaire, et du texte tout
entier de ses œuvres, est moins délicate. C'est tout d'abord
que les éditeurs des XVIIIe et XIXe siècles avaient leurs
propres normes, et que ces normes ne sont pas les nôtres. Ils

n'hésitaient jamais à supprimer un passage qu'ils trouvaient peu intéressant : ce sont précisément ces passages-là qui nous intéressent le plus par les petits détails de la vie intime ou quotidienne et que nos aïeux trouvaient au-dessous d'un grand homme. D'autre part, si Voltaire décrivait le même incident à plusieurs correspondants, les éditeurs souvent ne laissaient subsister qu'une des versions : tandis que pour nous les variantes entre les différentes narrations sont significatives et souvent passionnantes. Quand Voltaire était exceptionnellement préoccupé par tel ou tel événement — il l'était du reste toujours — il écrivait souvent une rapide succession de billets au même ou à différents correspondants : rien de plus facile que de les amalgamer en une seule 'grande' lettre, en ne sacrifiant rien que toute la saveur, toute la valeur psychologique et historique des textes authentiques.

Pour les suppressions dans un autre ordre d'idées, là encore c'est précisément l'inédit qui risque d'être ce qui est le plus intéressant. La démonstration détaillée de cette constatation dépasse le cadre d'une conférence, puisqu'elle appelle la citation d'un grand nombre de textes, mais certains principes sont évidents. Si, par exemple, au XVIIIᵉ siècle telle allusion capable d'offenser un personnage encore vivant est omise ; si sous la Restauration, des allusions incommodes à la monarchie sont supprimées par la censure dans ce qui reste du texte ; si au XIXᵉ siècle une censure moins visible mais d'autant plus efficace balaie tout ce qui est considéré comme spécialement obscène ou blasphématoire, il va de soi que le texte publié ne représente les paroles de Voltaire que d'une façon bien anémique. Il s'ensuit aussi que le nouveau Voltaire qu'on connaîtra demain sera un personnage infiniment plus vif, plus nuancé, plus humain qu'on ne se le représente aujourd'hui, capable d'un extraordinaire franc-parler, d'un langage vigoureux, de jeux d'esprit rabelaisiens qui n'épargnent ni les personnes les plus sacrées ni les plus éminentes. Bien sûr, une personnalité neutre n'effarouche pas la timidité des éditeurs.

Voltaire a souvent été accusé, je l'ai accusé moi-même,

d'avoir été trop sensible aux critiques. Les nouveaux apports le montrent dans ce sens en même temps meilleur et pire. Les textes non expurgés révèlent un langage encore plus violent contre les frelons de la littérature, mais ils révèlent aussi un Voltaire qui reçoit avec une patience et une docilité étonnantes les critiques bien intentionnées de ceux-là même qui étaient les moins qualifiés pour les lui offrir. Quant à son attitude envers les Desfontaines et les éditeurs flibustiers, il ne faut pas juger Voltaire d'après les normes du xxe siècle. Il n'y avait à son époque aucun droit d'auteur, ou presque. N'importe quel éditeur pouvait reproduire ses ouvrages criblés d'erreurs, et cela se fit non pas deux ou trois fois, mais pour des centaines d'éditions voltairiennes. N'importe qui pouvait voler son nom ou sa célèbre initiale, et par là couvrir les publications les plus ordurières et les plus sensationnelles. Par ailleurs, la diffamation n'était pas encore un concept juridique, et l'on disait et imprimait n'importe quoi contre un homme qu'on savait en défaveur à la Cour, et qui passait la plus grande partie de sa vie loin de Paris. Voltaire, l'homme le plus célèbre de l'Europe pendant un demi-siècle, a été obligé de supporter tout cela. Et l'on s'étonne que de temps en temps il ait réagi avec violence! Il faut être bien insensible, bien ignorant du monde, bien ignorant tout court, et bien dépourvu de l'expérience acquise par un homme dont le public s'occupe tant soit peu, pour faire de Voltaire l'objet d'accusations altièrement moralisatrices.

Un mot sur un élément des plus importants parmi les inédits que j'ai pu retrouver: les lettres adressées à Voltaire. Toutes les éditions en donnent, mais peu. J'en ajoute beaucoup, mais j'aimerais bien en retrouver beaucoup plus. Il est souvent possible de les raccorder avec les lettres de Voltaire auxquelles elles répondent. Nombreux sont les détails obscurs qui sont ainsi éclaircis, et le ton et la substance de ces lettres sont souvent hautement significatifs. Sur le plan personnel on peut se rendre compte avec quelle gentillesse Voltaire répond aux importunités de tel rimailleur qui lui demande de revoir ses

écrits; avec quelle générosité il réagit souvent aux requêtes
qu'on lui adresse, demandes d'argent, d'intervention, de lettres
de recommandation, de dons de ses publications; avec quelle
longanimité il supporte l'indifférence, la malhonnêteté même
de beaucoup de ses amis et de presque tous ses protégés; avec
quelle tolérance il pardonne aux secrétaires qui lui volent ses
manuscrits; combien son sens de la famille est fort, et avec
quelle libéralité il fait des pensions à tous, nièces, neveux,
petits-neveux, cousins éloignés. Voyez, je prends un exemple
parmi des centaines, telle lettre inédite d'Alembert, qui avait
mal compris un mot de Voltaire, et qui lui écrivit une lettre
d'une telle grossièreté, que je préfère ne pas la citer; la réponse
de Voltaire, également inédite, est remarquable; courtoisement,
amicalement, tranquillement, il répond point par point et il
termine: 'Je recommande l'union aux frères, e per fine, je vous
aime, révère, admire et regrette.' On voit que Voltaire pouvait
tout supporter, tout pardonner, sauf l'intolérance, l'injustice et
la malice.

### XIII

J'ai tenu à entrer dans ces quelques détails pour souligner que
la seule évaluation statistique ne permet guère de juger le
nouveau Voltaire qui émerge de cette édition. Celui, en effet,
qui n'examine que les lettres entièrement nouvelles, risque de
se tromper bien fâcheusement. Mais enfin il est indéniable que
ce qui est entièrement nouveau nous intéresse le plus. Comment vous donner la moindre idée de ce que représentent ces
10 000 lettres que j'ai l'immense honneur d'ajouter au *corpus*
voltairien? Par où commencer? Les 142 lettres d'amour à sa
nièce, retrouvées trop tard pour prendre leur place dans l'ordre
chronologique, et dont j'ai été obligé de faire un volume hors
série? lettres si tendres, si polissonnes qu'elles étonnent ceux
qui jugent Voltaire d'après les données devenues convention-
nelles. Les centaines de nouvelles lettres à d'autres correspondants déjà connus? Par exemple, la dernière édition des œuvres

de Voltaire contient autour de cent lettres à différents membres de la famille Tronchin, lettres imprimées pour la plupart dans des textes qui ne ressemblent que de très loin à ceux sortis de la plume de Voltaire. On connaît actuellement les manuscrits de 800 lettres aux Tronchin, lettres qui nous donnent une vaste quantité de renseignements des plus détaillés sur la vie et les activités de Voltaire aux Délices.

Un contraste encore plus frappant est fourni par la correspondance de Voltaire avec son éditeur Gabriel Cramer, celui qui en tout premier lieu l'amena à s'établir près du lac Léman. Les œuvres de Voltaire contiennent une douzaine de lettres à son 'caro Gabriele': j'en donne au delà de mille, lettres remplies de détails précieux sur les ouvrages de notre grand homme, ses méthodes de publication et de diffusion, et avant tout, sur leur date de composition respective.

L'une des plus intéressantes figures parmi les correspondants nouvellement découverts est celle, étrangement évanescente, de Charlotte Sophie von Aldenburg, Comtesse Bentinck, qui est à peine mentionnée même dans les biographies les plus détaillées de Voltaire. L'édition classique de ses œuvres ne contient pas une seule lettre d'elle ou à elle adressée: mais récemment trois cents des lettres que lui écrivit Voltaire ont émergé des archives de différentes branches de la famille Bentinck, avec quelques-unes de ses réponses. Elles nous obligent à une révision complète des années passées par Voltaire à Berlin et à Potsdam, à la cour de Frédéric. On supposait qu'il les avait passées plus ou moins dans la solitude, ponctuée surtout par les querelles alternant avec les réconciliations, par les coquetteries qui marquèrent ses curieuses relations avec le roi. Mais nous savons désormais que les activités de Voltaire étaient multiples et variées, quoiqu'elles lui laissaient le temps de voir Mme Bentinck presque chaque jour, et de lui écrire très fréquemment, fût-ce pour lui demander à emprunter son carrosse, pour accepter — mais plus souvent pour refuser — une invitation, ou pour se défendre de sa jalousie, en particulier envers une mystérieuse comtesse polonaise.

Et puis quoi encore ? Il y a une longue série de lettres détaillées à son petit-neveu d'Hornoy, une autre très longue à un
banquier dont le nom même ne paraît nulle part dans la littérature voltairienne, de nombreuses lettres à Constant d'Her-
menches, à son notaire Laleu, à Henri Rieu, à Manoël de
Végobre, à Labat, un nombre considérable de lettres adressées
à Voltaire par Cideville et qui révèlent en ce dernier un poète
inconnu de valeur modeste, mais certaine. Mais cette énumération devient ennuyeuse et ne pourrait être que fragmentaire,
même prolongée de beaucoup, puisqu'elle révèlerait 400 correspondants nouveaux. Laissons là ces généralités pour voir de
plus près Voltaire épistolier, c'est-à-dire, pour voir Voltaire.


## XIV

Il n'est pas question de prendre comme illustration une époque
générale de la vie de Voltaire, ni même une année, un mois, une
semaine. Penchons-nous plutôt sur une seule journée de la vie
de notre grand homme. Cette journée, je ne l'ai pas choisie dans
son étincelante jeunesse, ni dans sa maturité à Cirey ou en
Prusse, ni dans la période de transformation aux Délices,
période qui a vu la naissance de ce qu'on entend par le patri-
arche de Ferney. J'ai préféré l'une des époques les plus tristes,
les plus pénibles de sa vie. Il a soixante-quatorze ans, depuis
de longues années déjà il s'est complètement retiré à Ferney,
où il poursuit une activité acharnée, d'une part destructrice de
l'intolérance et de la religion, c'est-à-dire de la superstition ;
d'autre part constructive, bienfaisante, humaine. Il a toujours
chez lui un parent du côté maternel, paralytique et mourant ;
la petite Marie Corneille, son époux Dupuits, leurs enfants —
l'on sait que Voltaire a reçu chez lui la descendante du poète,
mais on oublie trop souvent qu'il l'a dotée, mariée, et toujours
gardée sous son toit — donc la famille Dupuits ; un jésuite
défroqué ; le jeune La Harpe et sa femme ; l'architecte Racle ;
l'avocat philosophe Christin ; le fidèle secrétaire Wagnière ; le
copiste Bigex ; quatorze officiers français qui font le blocus de

Genève. (Ils étaient d'un régiment dont le colonel, dit Voltaire dans une lettre inédite de mars 1768, 'est si occupé du service du roi, qu'étant de retour à Paris, il ne nous a pas seulement écrit un mot de remerciement'. Il est vrai que Voltaire ajoute: 'Ainsi en ont usé trois ou quatre cents Anglais, que nous avons très bien reçus, et qui sont si attachés à leur patrie qu'ils ne se sont jamais souvenus de nous.'[1] Je me suis permis de venger Voltaire de ces trois ou quatre cents de mes compatriotes.) Je disais donc, des officiers français; dans le château et ses dépendances, 60 domestiques et laboureurs (c'est le chiffre que donne Voltaire dans une lettre du 4 mars 1769); cinq, vingt, cinquante, cent hôtes de passage venus jouer la comédie, coucher, dîner, ou tout simplement contempler l'homme le plus célèbre du monde; et enfin celle qu'il ne faut surtout pas oublier, la veuve Denis, née Marie Louise Mignot, nièce, gouvernante et maîtresse du seigneur des lieux.

Nous sommes au mardi 1er mars 1768. J'aurais pu choisir tel ou tel jour pour lequel je suis parvenu à doubler, tripler ou quadrupler le nombre de lettres connues. Ç'aurait été trop facile. J'ai préféré une voie plus ardue, mais aussi plus révélatrice. En effet, pour ce mois de mars 1768 nous connaissions déjà trente-quatre lettres, et pour ce seul jour du premier du mois, pas moins de neuf. On se croyait bien renseigné sur les événements de cette période. En réalité, on la savait très mal, nous ne connaissions que la surface des choses — l'essentiel nous avait échappé. Il est vrai que pour ce mois de mars 1768, je ne connais qu'une vingtaine de lettres qu'on ne trouvera pas dans les éditions. Quantitativement, cet apport de nouvelles lettres, même pas 60%, est relativement faible dans le cadre voltairien où tout est gigantesque, quoique ce ne soient pas des inédits de la dernière banalité, puisque dans ce nombre il se trouve des épîtres adressées au Président Hénault, au chevalier de Rochefort, au pasteur Moultou, au ministre russe Vorontsov, au

---

[1] Jeu d'esprit bien sûr: les Anglais ont été très loin d'oublier Voltaire; voir Sir Gavin de Beer, 'Voltaire's British Visitors', *Studies on Voltaire and the Eighteenth Century* (Genève 1957), iv. 7–136.

pasteur Vernes, à l'éditeur Pierre Rousseau, à Alembert, sans
parler de deux lettres adressées par ce dernier à Voltaire, et
d'autres épîtres inédites de Mme Bentinck, d'Erlach von Rig-
gisberg, et d'autres.

Mais revenons au premier du mois il y a 191 ans. Les dissen-
sions entre Genève et Paris s'étaient un peu apaisées. Voltaire
était en quelque sorte un trait d'union entre les deux pays,
il s'efforçait d'encourager et de maintenir les relations amé-
liorées, et de ne rien faire, ce qui était moins commode, pour
réveiller les craintes et les soupçons. Or, quand il était le plus
tourmenté, le plus grave, Voltaire affectait de rire, et ce rire
s'appelait cette fois-ci la *Guerre civile de Genève*. Ce pamphlet
en vers avait été publié à l'insu de Voltaire, mais il était parvenu à mettre sous clé la partie la plus dangereuse, le deuxième
chant, où se trouvent quelques centaines de lignes du goût de :

> Près d'une église à Pierre consacrée,
> Très sale église, et de Pierre abhorrée,
> Qui brave Rome, hélas ! impunément,
> Sur un vieux mur est un vieux monument,
> Reste maudit d'une déesse antique,
> Du paganisme ouvrage fantastique,
> Dont les enfers animaient les accents
> Lorsque la terre était sans prédicants,
> Dieu quelquefois permet qu'à cette idole
> L'esprit malin prête encor sa parole.
> Les Genevois consultent ce démon
> Quand par malheur ils n'ont point de sermon.
> Ce diable antique est nommé l'Inconstance ;
> Elle a toujours confondu la prudence :
> Une girouette exposée à tout vent
> Est à la fois son trône et son emblême ;
> Cent papillons forment son diadème ; etc. etc.

On comprend que Voltaire n'ait pas voulu s'exposer, ni
exposer la France, aux réactions de la sensibilité genevoise à
de telles allusions. Or, voilà qu'un jour ce deuxième chant
s'imprime. Voltaire est à la dernière extrémité de la fureur et de

l'inquiétude, mais il reste juste. Posément, longuement, il fait ses enquêtes, et il en résulte avec certitude que le coupable est La Harpe, ce jeune littérateur qu'il avait reçu chez lui pendant de longs mois avec sa femme, comme ses enfants, et dont il avait chanté les louanges dans toutes ses lettres depuis deux ans. C'était lui qui avait volé le manuscrit à Ferney, qui l'avait emporté à Paris dans la même valise que les rouleaux de louis d'or que Voltaire avait l'habitude de glisser dans les bagages de ses protégés sur leur départ. Il y a pis. La Harpe avait été encouragé, soudoyé peut-être, par Mme Denis. Comment? On ne le saura jamais, bien que l'avidité vulgaire de cette femme et ses appétits, même à soixante ans, nous laissent deviner la réponse. Pour La Harpe, Voltaire lui pardonne avec une longanimité qui ne cesse d'étonner, comme il a toujours pardonné à ceux qui l'ont offensé sur le plan personnel. Non seulement il pardonne une action particulièrement déshonorante de la part d'un invité, d'un protégé; croyant au talent de La Harpe, et pour ne pas lui nuire — le jeune homme était très pauvre — Voltaire envoie aux journaux un démenti lavant La Harpe de tout soupçon. Et quelques mois plus tard seulement (10 mars 1769) il lui écrit: 'Mon cher panégyriste de Henri IV *et vitula tu dignus et hic*. Vous avez bien du talent en vers et en prose. Puisse-t-il servir à votre fortune comme il servira sûrement à votre réputation!'

Mais pour Mme Denis, dont ce n'était pas le premier délit du genre, il la met tout simplement à la porte. Elle fait l'innocente. Dans une lettre inédite (19 mai 1768) au voisin Henri Rieu, celui qui devait hériter les livres anglais de la bibliothèque de Voltaire, elle prétend ignorer la cause de la séparation. 'Tout ce que je puis vous dire c'est que malgré les boutades de Mon Oncle je l'aime toujours. Je n'impute point ses injustices à son cœur, parce qu'il les répare tant qu'il peut.' Et elle veut tout mettre au compte de la 'plate beste' le 'gesuite Adam'.

Voilà à peu près tout ce qu'on connaissait de cet incident, après tout assez plat et même sordide. Mais une leçon nous attend, une leçon qui nous enseignera une fois de plus, jamais assez, la nécessité impérieuse de la critique historique, des recherches documentaires.

Ecoutez une lettre inédite du secrétaire Jean Louis Wagnière adressée à Mme Denis 'chez Monsieur Tabareau, Directeur général des postes etc<sup>a</sup> à Lyon' — détail précieux déjà puisqu'il nous renseigne sur la route prise par Mme Denis pour retourner à Paris. Je vous lis la lettre en entier:

mardy au soir 1<sup>er</sup> Mars 1768

Madame,

J'ai cru que je serais tué à midy un quart par M<sup>r</sup> De Voltaire. J'ai été surpris après qu'il avait été pendant une heure seul avec père Adam qu'il m'ait dit que vous dormiez bien longtemps; je me suis écrié que vous étiez partie à dix heures, et que je croiais que Père Adam le lui avait dit. Il est entré dans toutes les fureurs contre moi, quoi que je lui aie dit que vous aviez tous frapé longtemps à ses portes qui étaient fermées des deux côtés, et que M<sup>r</sup> Dupuits avait voulu entrer trois fois chez lui. J'ai été si étourdi que j'en suis tout malade. Cependant il s'est un peu calmé.

Il a déchiré sa promesse de vingt mille livres qu'il vous donnera par an. Je crois qu'il vous en enverra une autre lorsque vous serez à Paris. M<sup>r</sup> Nicod a renvoié la procuration. Le cœur me battait un peu en la lui présentant. Il l'a parcourue tranquilement, et l'a mise dans son bureau en disant que cela était bon.

Voilà, Madame, comment s'est passée cette triste journée. Mon cœur vous souhaitte un heureux voiage, et j'espère que nous aurons le bonheur de vous revoir à Ferney.

Vous connaissez quel [est] mon profond respect, mon attachement et ma reconnaissance pour vous.

WAGNIERE

Deux mots seulement de commentaire sur cette lettre. Après la mort de son oncle, Mme Denis s'est conduite très mal, et avec une grande mesquinerie, envers le bon Wagnière. C'était, disait-elle, parce qu'il avait toujours été son ennemi et avait excité son oncle contre elle. D'après tout ce qu'on connaissait du caractère de Jean Louis, cette accusation méritait toutes les réserves. Nous avons maintenant la preuve de sa fausseté; en effet, tout cela n'était qu'un prétexte inventé et déshonorant.

La lettre de Wagnière ne trahit qu'une vraie amitié, et même, si l'on veut, quelque manque de discrétion vis-à-vis de son patron, en faveur de la nièce — conclusion du reste confirmée par d'autres lettres inédites que je publierai bientôt.

Ensuite, et c'est bien plus important, les mots 'Il a déchiré sa promesse de vingt mille livres' font peut-être entrevoir un Voltaire qui, dans l'excès de son amertume, décide de ne plus rien faire pour une femme à qui il a déjà donné une partie importante de sa fortune et qui a vécu à ses dépens — et fort luxueusement — depuis trente ans. On peut défendre ce geste, on peut le déplorer ou même le condamner, mais il faut surtout se dire que, quoique Wagnière ait certainement dit la vérité, après tout ni lui ni personne ne peut comprendre le vrai sens du geste. Et cette attitude de réserve est pleinement justifiée, car en réalité Voltaire a comblé Mme Denis de dons en partant, lui a augmenté sa pension, et ce n'est pas tout. En voici la preuve. Écoutez un bref extrait d'une autre lettre inédite, très longue, et dont le reste est trop plein d'allusions incompréhensibles sans de longs commentaires. Elle est toujours du même jour, adressée au futur Président d'Hornoy, fils du premier lit de la nièce cadette de Voltaire, pour lors Marquise de Florian. Même pour ce court extrait quelques gloses sont indispensables: le 'cher magistrat' c'est, comme je l'ai dit, le petit-neveu d'Hornoy; 'maman' c'est Mme Denis; Mme Dupuits c'est Marie Corneille; les affaires du Duc de Wurttemberg sont les revenus très irréguliers de la rente viagère que Voltaire avait achetée à ce prince; l'abbé Blet était l'homme d'affaires du Maréchal-Duc de Richelieu, chargé de la succession de la famille de Guise, lourdement endettée à Voltaire, qui avait arrangé le mariage de la princesse avec Richelieu en prêtant l'argent qui le rendait possible.

1er Mars 1768

Mon cher magistrat, maman, made Dupuits, feront bientôt ce que je voudrais faire, elles vous embrasseront. Il faut absolument que maman passe quelque temps à Paris pour ses gencives qui sont dans un état menaçant et il faudra que j'aille moi même mettre un ordre invariable dans mes affaires avec M^r Le Duc de Virtemberg, qui ne me devra jamais douze années comme les maréchaux de France.

Je vous prierai de partager entre elle et moi tout ce que me doit M^r Le Maréchal de Richelieu qui se monte à 27425^{ll} à ce que je crois. Il conviendra que le tout soit paié à la fois. Maman qui a beaucoup vécu avec lui se fera mieux paier qu'un sergent à verge. Il est vrai qu'elle n'est plus dans l'âge qui ouvre la bourse des Ducs et Pairs; mais une ancienne liaison est toujours respectée. Certainement vous viendrez tout deux à bout de dégraisser l'abbé Blet.

Admirez la discrétion, la loyauté, la maîtrise de soi de ce vieux monsieur écrivant à son petit-neveu sur la tante de ce dernier! Les gencives de Mme Denis! Quel homme merveilleux! Le beau siècle! Et n'oubliez pas que la dette du maréchal-duc que Voltaire offrait si gaillardement de partager avec sa nièce ferait quatorze millions de francs. Il est vrai que si Richelieu, mieux connu à l'époque sous le surnom élégant de 'père la maraude', avait dû récompenser de la sorte toutes ses anciennes liaisons, il lui aurait fallu pour y faire face plusieurs campagnes aussi fructueuses pour lui en butin que la dernière.

Et maintenant, c'est le moment de vérité. Vous allez savoir ce que ressentait Voltaire en réalité dans son for intérieur ce jour-là. Vous le saurez, en effet, grâce à la découverte d'une de ses plus remarquables lettres, en un sens peut-être la plus remarquable. Cette lettre fut adressée à sa nièce. Elle est restée inconnue jusqu'à ce jour: j'ai l'honneur de vous en offrir la primeur. En voici un large extrait:

à Ferney mardy 1^er mars [1768]<br>
à 2 heures après midy

Il y a une destinée sans doute, et souvent elle est bien cruelle. Je suis venu trois fois à votre porte, vous avez frappé à la mienne. J'ay voulu promener ma douleur dans le jardin. Il était dix heures, je mettais l'eguille sur dix heures au globe solaire, j'attendais que vous fussiez éveillée. J'ay rencontré monsieur Mallet. Il m'a dit qu'il était affligé de votre départ. J'ay jugé qu'il sortait de votre appartement. J'ay cru que vous dîneriez au châtau comme vous l'aviez dit. Aucun domestique ne m'a averti de rien, ils croiaient tous que j'étais instruit. J'ay fait venir Christin et père Adam. Nous nous sommes entretenus jusqu'à midy. Enfin je retourne chez vous. Je demande où vous êtes. Vaniere me dit, Eh quoy vous ne savez pas qu'elle est partie à dix heures! Je me retourne plus mort que vif vers p. Adam. Il me répond comme Vaniere, J'ay cru que vous le saviez! Sur le champ j'envoye chercher un cheval dans l'écurie. Il n'y avait personne. Ainsi dans la même maison avec vingt domestiques nous nous sommes cherchés sans nous voir. Je suis au désespoir, et cette obstination de mon malheur m'annonce un avenir bien sinistre. Je sçais que le moment de la séparation aurait été affreux: mais il est plus affreux encore que vous soyez partie sans me voir, tandis que nous nous cherchions l'un l'autre. J'ay envoyé vite chez madame Racle pour pleurer avec elle. Elle dîne avec Christin, Adam et son mari; et moy je suis très loin de dîner. Je me dévore et je vous écris. . . .

Vous verrez m^r de Choiseuil, de Richelieu, Dargental. Vous adoucirez mes malheurs; c'est encore là votre destinée. Vous réussirez à Paris dans vos affaires et dans les miennes, vous reverez votre frère et votre neveu. Si je meurs, je meurs tout entier à vous, si je vis ma vie est à vous. J'embrasse tendrement m^r et m^e du Pui. Je les aime, je les regrette, j'ay le cœur percé.

Telle est, en partie, la lettre adressée par Voltaire à cette nièce qui lui devait tout, qui l'avait cent fois trahi dans ses affections, qui s'était rendue coupable de torts abominables, et qui venait de le quitter sans un mot d'adieu après quarante années d'amitié et d'amour. Telle est la lettre de cet homme dont ses adversaires, que leur croyance devrait inviter, je ne dis même pas à plus de charité, mais à plus de justice, ont voulu faire un monstre rancunier et sans cœur. N'insistons pas.

Il est donc deux heures, deux heures et demie de l'après-midi, le premier mars 1768. Voltaire, comme le plus commun des mortels, ne trouve qu'une consolation à son chagrin: il se plonge dans le travail, avec une noble et triste sérénité. Le brave Wagnière a dû se coucher ce soir-là avec une jolie crampe des écrivains!

On trouve d'abord ce jour-là une correspondance avec le Résident de France à Genève, Pierre Michel Hennin : je dis bien 'correspondance', car quatre fois, et peut-être même six fois ce mardi, le cheval du courrier a fait le parcours entre Ferney et l'hôtel de France à Genève. Le matin, Voltaire avait déjà écrit une longue lettre pour assurer Hennin qu'une certaine 'Languedochienne avec ses beaux yeux' ('Languedochienne' n'est ni un calembour ni une allusion méchante — le mot se prononçait ainsi à l'époque) n'avait pas pu voir le second chant de la *Guerre civile*, et que c'était La Harpe qui était coupable de l'infidélité ; il demande aussi les gazettes. Hennin les lui envoie, ajoutant 'Quand vous voudrez n'être pas seul je vous prie de me le faire savoir. Vous ne devez pas douter du plaisir que j'aurai de vous prouver en tout temps et de toutes manières mon dévouement.' Le même soir Voltaire renvoie les gazettes à son 'cher ministre' : 'Maman est partie, me voylà hermite. Vous savez que le diable le devint quand il fut vieux. Mais quoy qu'on dise, je ne suis pas diable.'

Entre temps c'est une véritable avalanche de lettres. Voici un mot à son 'divin ange' le Comte d'Argental, pour lui envoyer une petite publication que Voltaire désavoue, bien sûr, mais qui se trouve pourtant dans ses œuvres sous le titre de *Lettre de l'archevêque de Cantorbéri à l'archevêque de Paris* : c'est une défense du *Bélisaire* de Marmontel contre les foudres de l'in-tolérance. C'est à cela qu'il fait allusion quand il dit au cher d'Argental qu'il brave les foudres de Rome pour lui écrire. Quant au voyage de Mme Denis et des Dupuits, il est néces-saire. 'Que ne pui-je en être ?' Mais dans cette lettre à son ami le plus intime, Voltaire ne fait aucune allusion à La Harpe. Pourquoi ? C'est précisément parce que le loyal d'Argental aurait eu une vive et dangereuse réaction. Voltaire s'explique quelques semaines plus tard (16 avril 1768) dans une lettre inédite :

Vous demandez, mon cher ange, qu'on vous ouvre son cœur.... Je ne vous ai point parlé de l'avanture de Laharpe, qui je crois n'est guères connu de vous, et à qui d'ailleurs je ne veux point faire de peine, et qui n'a jamais eu intention de me nuire, quelque tort qu'il ait pu avoir avec moi. Il est jeune, il est pauvre, il est marié; il a besoin d'apui, je n'ai pas voulu lui ravir vôtre estime.

Voici une lettre au jeune Chabanon, dont l'*Eudoxie* avait été écrite à Ferney, et amplement corrigée depuis par notre grand homme:

Maman verra donc Eudoxie avant moy, mon cher confrère. Elle part pour Paris, elle fera madame Dupuis juge si on joue mieux la comédie à Paris qu'à Ferney.... Elle va arranger sa santé, ses affaires et les miennes. Tout cela s'est délabré pendant vingt ans qu'elle a été loin de Paris.... Voilà Ferney redevenu un désert comme il l'était avant que j'y eusse mis la main. Je quitte Melpomene pour Ceres et Pomone. Braves jeunes gens cultivez les baux arts, et gorgez vous de plaisirs, j'ay fait mon temps.

Voici une lettre au charmant Dorat. La Harpe en effet avait déjà été coupable d'une première indiscrétion: il avait envoyé à Paris de Ferney une petite flèche épigrammatique au gracieux poète:

Bon Dieu, que cet auteur est triste en sa gaîté!
Bon Dieu, qu'il est pesant dans sa légèreté!
Que ses petits écrits ont de longues préfaces!
Ses fleurs sont des pavôts, ses ris sont des grimaces.
Que l'encens qu'il prodigue est plat et sans odeur!
Il est, si je l'en crois, un heureux petit-maître;
Mais, si j'en crois ses vers, qu'il est triste d'être
Ou sa maîtresse ou son lecteur!

Fort bien! pas du tout du style de notre grand homme, mais inévitablement à lui attribué. Or Voltaire préférait façonner ses propres flèches, et surtout en choisir les cibles, et il ne tenait pas du tout à offenser le jeune Dorat. C'est pourquoi il entre dans de longues explications et protestations d'innocence:

En un mot, Monsieur, je suis trop vrai, et j'ai trop de franchise pour n'en être pas cru quand j'ai juré à mad^e Necker sur mon honneur que je n'avais nulle part à cette tracasserie. C'est à vous à savoir quels sont vos ennemis. Pour moi je ne le suis pas. J'ai été très affligé de cette imposture. J'ai des preuves en main qui me justifieraient pleinement [etc.].

(Cette Mme Necker, à qui Voltaire a juré son innocence, est celle qui venait de donner naissance à la petite Anne Louise Germaine, plus tard Mme de Staël.)

Voici une lettre à François Louis Henri Leriche, directeur-général des domaines à Besançon. Il se plaint que ses paquets ont été 'impudemment saisis à S<sup>t</sup> Claude'; il proteste 'qu'il n'est rien que l'insolente inquisition de certaines gens ne se soit permis contre les lois du royaume'; et il conclut: 'Il se fait une très grande révolution dans les esprits en Italie et en Espagne. Le monde entier secoue les chaînes du fanatisme, mais l'ombre du chevalier de La Barre crie en vain vengeance contre ses assassins.'

Voici une lettre au Conseil suprême de Montbéliard, fief du Duc de Wurttemberg, qui lui avait vendu une rente viagère. Or le duc et ses hommes d'affaires trouvent fort étonnant et même révoltant qu'un poète s'attende à être payé régulièrement et ponctuellement. Voltaire est obligé de demander vingt fois, de faire des menaces, et même de citer le duc devant la cour. Cette fois il se contente d'apitoyer le Conseil suprême: 'Je me trouve dans un état forcé; et dans un abîme dont je ne pourais sortir sans les arrangements que vous avez bien voulu prendre. J'attends les délégations et les billets.' Et il ajoute: 'Si j'étais seul, soiez bien persuadés, Messieurs, que je ne vous impor- tunerais pas; mais j'ai une famille nombreuse qui n'a pour vivre que les rentes en question.'

Voici une lettre au Duc de Richelieu, un de ses plus anciens amis, pour annoncer l'arrivée à Paris de Mme Denis. 'Ma fille adoptive Corneille l'accompagne à Paris, où elle verra mas- sacrer les pièces de son grand oncle. Pour moy je reste dans mon désert. Il faut bien qu'il y ait quelqu'un qui prenne soin du ménage de campagne. C'est ma consolation.' Et il ajoute: 'Je me regarde déjà comme un homme mort quoy que j'aye égaié mon agonie autant que je l'ay pu.'

Voici une lettre au chevalier Jacques de Rochefort d'Ally pour le remercier d'un présent. 'Vous m'avez envoyé, monsieur, du vin de Champagne quand je suis à la tisane; c'est envoyer une fille à un châtré.'

Voici une lettre au pasteur Jacob Vernes; elle est exceptionnelle celle-là, en ce 1er mars, car elle est courte, ce qui me permet de la citer en entier:

Prêtre d'un Dieu père de tous les hommes, prédicateur de la raison, prêtre tolérant, si vous voulez avoir le militaire philosophe de feu St Hiacinthe il est chez votre illustre et digne ami Mr de Moultou qui vous le prêtera sur ce billet.

Avez vous vu le sermon prêché à Bale? Je le crois de votre petit frère.

Madame Denis va à Paris pour les affaires temporelles. Quand viendrez vous traitter icy les spirituelles?

Liber libera liberrime.

Inutile d'ajouter que le petit frère, auteur du *Sermon prêché à Bâle le premier jour de l'an 1768, par Josias Rosette, ministre du saint évangile*, sermon pour rendre grâce à dieu 'du plus grand événement qui ait signalé le siècle où nous vivons', c'est-à-dire l'expulsion des jésuites, que ce petit frère, donc, s'appelait Voltaire.

Sur ce, avec cette treizième lettre, laissons Voltaire se reposer de ses émotions et de ses travaux ce mardi, 1er mars 1768.

Il n'aurait été que trop facile d'entrer dans de larges développements sur Voltaire philosophe, Voltaire poète, Voltaire homme de théâtre, et ainsi de suite. Dans tous ces domaines, et vingt autres, il y a de nouveaux apports, souvent très importants, dans les milliers de lettres inédites que j'ai l'honneur de publier, des modifications à faire à l'image traditionnelle du grand homme. Mais ce n'était pas là le but de mes conférences. J'ai essayé plutôt de vous faire voir le vrai Voltaire en vous le montrant dans son intimité, en vous introduisant chez lui comme dans le salon d'un ancien ami: rarement est-il donné de suivre une journée d'un grand homme du passé dans un tel

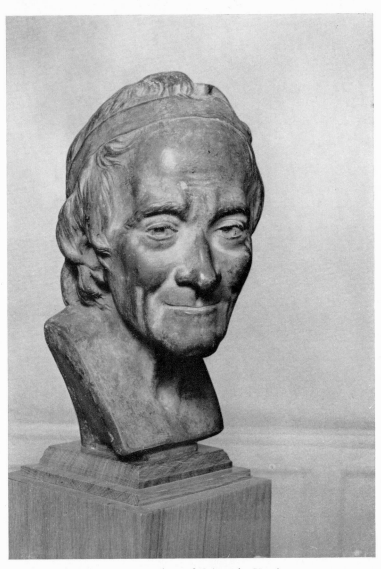

5. Terra-cotta bust of Voltaire by Houdon

6. Head of the statue

détail et dans un épanchement aussi complet. Et si, selon le mot
de Valéry, Voltaire 'se fait admirer, adorer, abhorrer, haïr et
vénérer, bâtonner, couronner, avec une sorte de maîtrise
encyclopédique' — je pense, moi, que pris ainsi sur le vif, il se
fait en plus et surtout aimer.

# The *Institut et Musée Voltaire* and its *Collections*[1]

*to Bernard Gagnebin*

WHEN I founded the Institute it was far from my intention to add just another museum to the many establishments already devoted to the memory of great men. My intention was rather, as in fact the name Institute clearly indicates, to found a centre of research devoted to the great man who personifies a great intellectual revolution and all the characteristics of an entire age. It is reasonable, therefore, to begin with an account of the activities of the Institute (founded in 1952, and formally opened in 1954), in so far as they are shown by publications, and leaving aside lectures, meetings, and exhibitions.

## I

A word to start with about Voltaire's presence in the neighbourhood of Geneva. We know that he spent several years at Les Délices before becoming the patriarch of Ferney. Relatively little importance is ordinarily attached to the Délices period, which is often regarded as a transitional one. This is a mistake, because in fact it was during the years 1755 to 1759, when Voltaire lived almost exclusively at Les Délices (he lived there intermittently until 1765), that what is commonly called Voltaire's philosophy acquired its definitive form.

After the sordid episode at Frankfurt Voltaire spent nearly two years, mainly in Alsace and at Lyon, looking for somewhere to live permanently. He would have preferred to return to Paris, but the king let it be known that he was *persona non*

[1] Taken from the guide to the Institute.

*grata*. But Voltaire did not want to exile himself by going as far away as England. On the other hand he knew the Low Countries well—too well to go back there. No German-speaking province could be considered out of reach of Frederick's unscrupulous attacks. The authorities in Berne showed no great eagerness to welcome him. As for Italy, without doubt he regarded that as too close to the great source of infection. With the possibilities thus narrowed down, Voltaire finally fixed on the 'microscopic' republic of Geneva, and in March 1755 took up his abode at Saint-Jean, at the very gates of the city.

During all this time, Voltaire was in a state of deep depression: he had been betrayed by Frederick, the future looked dark, and he began to despair of ever having a roof over his head. Now, setting up house at Les Délices, he suddenly recovered his good humour, and it seemed that all the necessary conditions combined for a brilliant renewal of his happiness and creative activity. This was not to be, so far as the happiness is concerned, for his outburst of euphoria, the poem he wrote at Les Délices, a little too soon, in praise of liberty and friendship, immediately drew fresh persecutions down on him, and for a trivial, even ridiculous reason: too friendly a reference to a Savoyard pope of the fifteenth century. The reference was taken amiss by the Court of Savoy, and the Genevan authorities obediently condemned the poem.

This incident was followed by others, by the Seven Years War, by what seemed to Voltaire a general recrudescence of human folly, and above all by the Lisbon earthquake of 1755. Towards 1758 this all began to boil up, and it exploded in the form of *Candide*, published at the beginning of 1759. With the publication of this book Voltaire took up a philosophical position from which he was never to depart. This position can be briefly defined thus: man has nothing to hope for from any other power than his own; he must improve himself by his own efforts; he must find his own salvation; he must cultivate his garden.

It was, in short, during his stay at Les Délices that Voltaire put off the old man, and put on the new. It was the most decisive moment in his long life.

## II

The Institute's chief publication is an edition of Voltaire's correspondence, based for the first time on original sources, even, in nine cases out of ten, on manuscripts. This edition contains twice the number of letters given in the previous collection of the correspondence, but the qualitative aspect is just as important as the quantitative. In fact, practically all Voltaire's letters were previously known only in inaccurate transcriptions; often, even, unimaginably falsified and distorted. Restorations and corrections run into literally tens of thousands. *Voltaire's Correspondence* publishes the texts in the French original, naturally, but the notes are in English. As a rule the notes on each letter fall into four parts: (1) the manuscript sources are given in detail; (2) if the letter was previously published, even if only in extract, the first edition is given, together with any other editions that may throw light on the text; (3) textual notes, variants, &c.; (4) explanatory notes—historical, biographical, philological, &c.

It must be emphasized that this edition is not limited to letters by Voltaire himself: it includes all his correspondence. Many letters written to him by others have been discovered, and it is often these that give us important new information.

*Voltaire's Correspondence*, which is helped by a valued grant from the Swiss national fund for scientific research, comprises at present seventy-four volumes, in which are published 15,268 letters, addressed to a thousand correspondents. The work reproduces the title-pages of the original or other important editions of nearly all Voltaire's works, and prints numerous facsimiles, maps, pictures, portraits, &c.

The Institute also publishes a bilingual Anglo-French review, *Studies on Voltaire and the Eighteenth Century*; twenty volumes have appeared so far. Some of these are devoted to a single long study: *Berthier's Journal de Trévoux and the philosophes*, by John N. Pappas; *L'Anti-Machiavel, par Frédéric, roi de Prusse, édition critique avec les remaniements de Voltaire pour les deux versions*, by Charles Fleischauer; *Voltaire's Candide: analysis of a classic*, by William F. Bottiglia; *Voltaire's Catalogue of his Library at Ferney*, by G. R. Havens and N. L. Torrey; *Poetic Genesis: Sébastien Mercier into Victor Hugo*, by H. Temple Patterson; *La Genèse et la rédaction de l'*Emile, by Peter J. Jimack; *Voltaire's Literary Career from 1728 to 1750*, by P. M. Conlon; *La Propagande philosophique dans les tragédies de Voltaire*, by Ronald S. Ridgway; Diderot, *Est-il bon? est-il méchant?*, critical edition by Jack Undank; *L'Abbé Desfontaines et son rôle dans la littérature de son temps*, by Thelma Morris.

The other volumes contain hitherto unpublished texts of Alembert, Baculard d'Arnaud, Breteuil, Comte de Bulkeley, Condorcet, Count Gustav Filip Creutz, Diderot, Mme Du Deffand, Falconet, Flaubert, Frederick II, Mme de Graffigny, Hénault, Holbach, La Harpe, Baron Carl Fredrick Scheffer, Suard, Mme Suard, Voltaire; articles, essays, and notes on Boulainvilliers, Pierre Cuppé, Jean Auguste Delmas, Diderot, Du Bos, Mme Du Châtelet, l'*Encyclopédie méthodique*, Falconet, John Fiske, Flaubert, Frederick II, Fréret, Mme de Graffigny, Hobbes, Houdon, La Mettrie, Maupertuis, Montesquieu, Pilati di Tassulo, Prévost, the *Recueil philosophique et littéraire*, Rousseau, Saint-Pierre, Saurin, the Suard family, James Thomson, Voltaire; among the contributors are Max I. Baym, Alfred J. Bingham, L. A. Boiteux, J. Th. de Booy, E. R. Briggs, J. D. Candaux, Enzo Caramaschi, Margaret Chenais, P. M. Conlon, Lester G. Crocker, Sir Gavin de Beer, Paul Dimoff, René Duthil, C. E. Engel, Rita Falke, Renzo de Felice, Madeleine Fields, Joseph G. Fucilla, Bernard Gagnebin, Peter Gay, Ronald Grimsley, Oscar A. Haac, F. G. Healey, A. C. Keys, R. A. Leigh, Ruth T. Murdoch, Leif Nedergaard-Hansen, Jean A. Perkins, Merle L. Perkins, René Pomeau,

Gunnar von Proschwitz, Georges Roth, Bertrand Russell, Jean Seznec, Robert Shackleton, Renée Simon, Leland Thielemann, Virgil W. Topazio, Norman L. Torrey, Jack Undank, Franco Venturi, Jérôme Vercruysse, Françoise Weil.

Many volumes contain supplements to the previously published volumes of *Voltaire's Correspondence.*

The Institute has also printed two volumes of *Voltaire's Notebooks*; a *Table de la bibliographie de Voltaire par Bengesco*, by Jean Malcolm; *D'Holbach's moral philosophy: its background and development*, by Virgil W. Topazio; a two-volume edition of the *Lettres de la marquise Du Châtelet*; the *Lettres d'amour de Voltaire à sa nièce* (published in collaboration with the Librairie Plon); and the *Discours prononcé par Theodore Besterman à l'inauguration de l'Institut et Musée Voltaire.*

### III

Such results could have been achieved only after long and thorough preparation, and the gathering together of a huge number of documents, so that much of the necessary research for all these publications, and especially for the edition of the correspondence, could be done within the walls of the Institute. The documents include first of all a great number of photographic reproductions (photographs, photocopies, enlarged microfilms), and in particular about 250,000 pages of reproductions of letters, gathered, not without difficulty and expense, from 300 archives, libraries, and private collections from practically all over the world. All these documents are arranged in chronological order, with various card-indexes—bibliographical, alphabetical, &c. The photographic reproductions are gradually being bound. When all the work is completed the collection will consist of about 200 large volumes.

The Institute also possesses the originals of several hundred letters published or to be published in *Voltaire's Correspondence*. Naturally most of these are letters by Voltaire himself, but there are many others, mostly letters addressed to him. These are signed by Algarotti, the Marquis d'Argenson, Argental, the Comtesse d'Argental, Benedict XIV, Bouhier, Chauvelín, Mme Denis, the Marquise Du Châtelet, Sébastien Dupont, the Cardinal de Fleury, the Marquise de Florian, Frederick II, Helvétius, La Beaumelle, Le Blanc, Mayáns y Siscar, the Maréchal de Noailles, Mme de Puisieux, the Duc de Richelieu, Rousset de Missy, Saint-Hyacinthe, the Duchesse de Saxe-Gotha, Tournemine, Queen Ulrika of Sweden, Voisenon, &c.

As we know, after Voltaire's death Beaumarchais embarked on and brought to a brilliant conclusion an admirable edition of Voltaire's works, the Kehl edition. What distinguishes this edition from the various collections of Voltaire's work that appeared during his lifetime is that for the first time it included his correspondence. Several hundred letters had appeared during his lifetime, it is true, but the Kehl edition is the first to present a sizeable and organized selection (not very well organized, I admit) of the letters which have contributed so much to Voltaire's reputation. Another thing that contributes to the importance of the Kehl edition is that this first edition of the letters, which appeared in 1785-9, remained until 1953, apart from a few minor selections, also the last edition to be based on the manuscripts. Beaumarchais and his collaborators had access to the original letters, and those that could not be retained were faithfully transcribed by amanuenses. It was these copies that were used for the work of editing, suppressing, adapting, and so on, imposed by the taste of the day and the demands of the authorities. Nearly 3000 of these manuscripts, with notes by Condorcet and others, survived in the archives of the Beaumarchais family, and now form part of the Institute's collections. A more detailed description of this valuable collection can be found in Appendix 7 of volume i of *Voltaire's Correspondence*.

Unfortunately Voltaire's library, including a large number of manuscripts, was after his death sold with indecent haste to Catherine II, by Voltaire's niece Mme Denis. As a result, his literary manuscripts are as rare as his letters are many. The Institute possesses a volume containing the original manuscripts of the *Dialogues d'Evhémère*, the *Commentaire sur l'Esprit des lois de Montesquieu*, the *Edits de sa majesté Louis XVI pendant l'administration de M. Turgot*, the *Résumé du Procès verbal d'Abbeville*, and a manuscript of *Irène*, in the hand of the faithful Wagnière, with interesting corrections and annotations by Voltaire.

The Institute also owns an album containing examples of Voltaire's handwriting at different periods of his life, prepared by Beaumarchais for the Marquise de Villette (the Beautiful and Good); a manuscript of the *Pucelle*, in the hand of Mme Denis; and numerous personal documents, diplomas, business papers, &c. For some details of these see 'The Manuscripts of the Institut et Musée Voltaire', *Studies on Voltaire and the Eighteenth Century* (Genève 1958), vi. 291–3.

But the Institute's manuscript collections are not strictly limited to Voltaire: rather, they cover the whole period that he symbolizes. Thus there is an extensive collection of Saint-Lambert's letters, Linguet's unpublished memoirs, several volumes of satirical songs, with music, the Suard archives, &c. The last-mentioned archives include letters written by Agasse, Alembert, the Duc de Bassano, Beauharnais, Joseph Bonaparte, Condorcet, Cuvier, Mme Du Deffand, Garat, Mme d'Houdetot, Mme Geoffrin, La Fayette, La Harpe, Mlle de Lespinasse, Mallet Du Pan, Marmontel, Michaud, the Comte de Mollé, Morellet, Naigeon, Necker, Mme Necker, Nodier, Panckoucke, Saint-Chamand, Saurin, Mme de Staël, Suard, Mme Suard, Wilkes, and many others.

## IV

The printed works, which at present number 10,000, consist of editions of Voltaire's books, writings about him, and writings of or about the eighteenth century in France.

As to Voltaire's own works, there is first of all an almost

complete series of collected editions, of considerable bibliographical interest. These editions range from that of 1728 to
the last one in 1877–85, and from that of Didot, in three
volumes and microscopic print, to several eighteenth-century
editions in a hundred volumes. The collected editions alone
occupy about fifty shelves, without counting selections and the
collected editions of poems, plays, stories, and correspondence.
The books and articles in which letters, or even a single letter,
by Voltaire appeared for the first time run into hundreds.

Separate editions of the works are, of course, very numerous,
because my intention was to collect together all the old editions,
all modern editions of any interest, and all translations into
foreign languages. These last include translations into Bulga-
rian, Czech, Danish, Dutch, English, German, Hungarian,
Icelandic, Italian, Japanese, Latin, Polish, Portuguese, Roma-
nian, Russian, and Slovak. But it is impossible to give any
idea, even a general one, of the richness of the Institute's printed
resources. It must suffice to mention that they include more
than 240 French eighteenth-century editions unknown to
Voltaire's great bibliographer, Georges Bengesco. Most of
these editions are described with full bibliographical details in
my essay, 'Some eighteenth-century Voltaire editions unknown
to Bengesco', *Studies on Voltaire and the Eighteenth Century*
(1959), viii. 123–242.

The last category of printed works includes a reasonably
complete collection of all that is necessary for the study of
Voltaire in relation to his age: first of all bibliographies, biographies, iconographies, studies on him, to the number of
nearly a thousand. His contemporaries are represented by their
collected works and by critical editions. Certain of them, such
as Diderot, Frederick II, Rousseau, &c., are very fully represented. In addition, there are nearly all the memoirs, biographies, and correspondences of the period, and a selection
of works on the history, foreign relations, finances, literature,
theatre, art, &c., of France in the eighteenth century. Finally
there are more or less complete collections of selected periodicals:

*Annales Prince de Ligne, Annales de la Société Jean-Jacques Rousseau, Cahiers de l'Association internationale des études françaises, French Studies, Journal of the History of Ideas, Modern Language Notes, Modern Language Review, Publications of the Modern Language Association of America, Revue d'histoire littéraire de la France, Revue de littérature comparée, Romanic Review, Studi francesi, The Year's Work in Modern Language Studies, Zeitschrift für französische Sprache und Literatur,* &c., as well as several sets of contemporary newspapers and periodicals.

There is already an author catalogue of printed works. A subject catalogue and a chronological catalogue are also in preparation. Because of research actively in progress, it is almost impossible for us to lend, but students are always welcome at Les Délices.

v

I come now to the museum of the Institute, which has grown up round the little gallery founded at Les Délices in 1945 by a group devoted to Geneva's intellectual and artistic heritage. Since then it has been further enriched by gifts from generous patrons in Geneva and elsewhere. During the reconstruction of Les Délices, carried out by the City of Geneva to provide for the Institute's needs, Voltaire's salon has been restored almost completely to what it was two centuries ago. A large gallery has also been installed with show-cases exhibiting a choice of manuscripts, and rare and interesting editions, medals, statuettes, &c. Particularly important among the rich iconography that the Institute possesses in the gallery, the salon, the library, and here and there throughout, are a magnificent bust in red terra-cotta by Houdon, a portrait of the young Voltaire by Largillière, another by Nattier of Mme Du Châtelet, a statuette of Voltaire by Lucas de Montigny, two fine heads of Voltaire and Rousseau by an unknown hand, several portraits by Huber, a group of three interesting paintings of Cirey, a picture of

Geneva by Malgo, showing the view from Les Délices at that time, a series of three water-colours painted on the terrace at Les Délices, and many other portraits and views, &c., together with thousands of engravings and other prints. A catalogue of representations of Voltaire is being prepared, but will not be ready for publication for some years.

In the lovely oval salon, with its contemporary panelling, which forms the entrance-hall, stands the most important piece of all: the original terra-cotta, executed by Houdon for Beaumarchais, of the great seated Voltaire.

For the history of the house, see Lucien Fulpius's study, *Une Demeure historique: les Délices de Voltaire* (Genève 1943).

# The Terra-cotta Statue of Voltaire made by Houdon for Beaumarchais[1]

*to the memory of Jacob Epstein*

## I

VOLTAIRE, the supreme genius of the eighteenth century, Houdon, its greatest sculptor: the encounter of these two marvels could not but engender a dazzling phenomenon. And indeed every bust or statuette of Voltaire by Houdon is a revelation of the sculptor's art and insight at their highest. What remains to be said of his life-size statue of Voltaire seated? All are agreed that this masterly creation represents the summit of Houdon's work.[2] It is 'unquestionably one of the masterpieces of Houdon, if not indeed simply his masterpiece'.[3] To say that the seated Voltaire is the 'masterpiece of ironic sculpture' would be banal. 'Here we have one of those sublime creations, one of those perfect harmonies which are not encountered ten times in ten centuries. There is condensed in it all that can be conceived for the perfection of a human masterpiece.'[4]

Apart of course from casts and late copies, his great work is known in the following forms: (1) the original plaster in the Bibliothèque nationale (the pedestal of which contains Voltaire's heart); (2) another plaster (possibly a replica), which was for-

---

[1] This paper has been revised from a first version in French, published in *Genava* (Genève décembre 1957), N.S. v. 149–59; I owe thanks to the Musée d'Art et d'Histoire for their hospitality.

[2] Louis Réau, *Houdon* (Paris 1930), p. 44.

[3] Georges Giacometti, *La Vie et l'œuvre de Houdon* (Paris [1929]), ii. 270.

[4] Louis Gonse, *Les Chefs-d'œuvre des musées de France* (Paris 1904), ii. 266.

merly in the Coty collection;[1] (3) a replica in the Musée Fabre
at Montpellier; (4) the marble at the Comédie Française; (5) the
marble in the Hermitage.[2]

The Montpellier replica is an interesting oddity from a technical point of view, for it is made up of several pieces, partly in
plaster, partly in terra-cotta. As for the Hermitage marble, it is
a copy by Houdon, or at any rate from his studio, of that given
to the Comédie Française by Voltaire's niece Mme Denis.

To these five statues must now be added a sixth, equalled in
importance only by the Bibliothèque nationale plaster; this
'new' terra-cotta is as remarkable for its unique beauty and its
technical interest as for its remarkable provenance.

II

The boulevard Saint-Antoine, renamed boulevard Beaumarchais in 1881, leads to the site of the Bastille. The corner now
occupied by numbers 2 to 20 was formerly part of the boulevard ditch, which later became a long, narrow plot of waste
ground. Beaumarchais acquired it 26 June 1787,[3] and con-
structed on it a fine and even magnificent house,[4] to the designs
of Paul Guillaume Lemoine. The windows of this unusual
house overlooked the Bastille. The garden was designed by
François Joseph Belanger,[5] and in it were to be admired

[1] According to François Spar (*Connaissance des arts*, Paris 15 août 1953,
p. 5) it found no purchaser at the Coty sale.

[2] Houdon was paid 20,000 *livres* (about $20,000 today) for his marble;
see Houdon's letter in Paul Vitry, 'La Statue de la *Philosophie* de Houdon',
*Archives de l'art français* (Paris 1907), N.S. i. 214.

[3] A copy of the document, in the Archives de la Seine, has been published
by A[lbert] C[aillet], 'La Maison de Beaumarchais', *La Cité* [Paris janvier
1905], iv. 319–21.

[4] See J[ean] C[harles] Krafft and Nicolas Ransonnette, *Plans, coupes, éléva-
tions des plus belles maisons et des hôtels construits à Paris et dans les environs*
(Paris [c. 1810]), plates 23, 24, 86 (salon); and G. Lenôtre [Théodore Gosselin],
*Les Quartiers de Paris pendant la Révolution* (Paris 1896), plates 5 and 11.

[5] [Mlle] A. Loiseau, the architect's pupil and friend, unfortunately adds
no details to this bare fact in her little biography of Belanger, published under
the sole title of *Nécrologie* [Paris 1818], p. 10; this pamphlet has been reprinted
in the *Revue universelle des arts* (Paris &c. 1865), xxii. 95–101.

terraces, a bridge, monuments, the tomb intended to receive
Beaumarchais's remains, and pavilions, including one dedicated to the glory of Voltaire, and containing his life-size statue
by Houdon. So numerous were the curious who wanted to see
this garden and all it contained that Beaumarchais was obliged
to have tickets of admission engraved. A water-colour[1] by
Belanger himself shows the cupola of the temple dedicated to
Voltaire, a kiosk the details of which can be seen on an engraving by Gautier.[2]

Beaumarchais died in this house in 1799. Legrand and
Landon, who reproduce its foundation plans and the elevation
of one of its façades, describe the house as it appeared in 1805.
They confirm the survival of the Voltaire garden-house: 'It is
decorated internally by fourteen Ionic columns, externally by
two Doric columns, over which can be read the inscription:
*Il ôte aux nations le bandeau de l'erreur.*' However, at this date
the statue of Voltaire had been removed to the antichamber of
the drawing-room.[3] According to the plan of the first floor the
great drawing-room had two antichambers, one of them oval.
It is perhaps permissible to hope that the statue, now placed for
good in the oval antichamber of the Délices, stood formerly in
Beaumarchais's oval room.

The house was spared by the Revolution,[4] and was still
intact under the Directory, together with the Voltaire pavilion
and his statue.[5] In 1818 the property was bought back by the city
of Paris from the heirs of Beaumarchais, and soon afterwards the
house was demolished and the site broken up.[6] Some ruins of

[1] Bibliothèque nationale, Cabinet des estampes, Collection Destailleur,
Ve 53c, i. 111.

[2] Bibliothèque nationale, Cabinet des estampes, Va 294: Topographie de
la France, Seine, Paris, xi^e arrondissement, 43^e quartier, i. [19].

[3] J[acques] G[uillaume] L[egrand] and C[harles] P[aul] Landon, *Description
de Paris et de ses édifices* (Paris 1808), ii. 11. 32.

[4] Edmond and Jules de Goncourt, *Histoire de la société française pendant
le Directoire* (troisième édition, Paris 1864), p. 59.

[5] Ibid., p. 58.

[6] Marquis [Félix] de Rochegude and Maurice Dumolin, *Guide pratique à
travers le vieux Paris* (nouvelle édition, Paris [1923]), p. 129.

the garden-house still survived about the year 1840, when the young Victorien Sardou played in what remained of the garden.[1] The Voltaire temple, which was at the extreme end of the property, protected by its wall, still stood.[2]

Not long afterwards the demolitions were completed, and the statue, the exceptional interest of which had no doubt been forgotten, was given shelter by one Fossard, house-demolisher, whose yard was at 392 rue de Belleville. M. Paul Gouvert was able to obtain a first-hand statement about this chapter in the history of the statue from M. Puard, Fossard's nephew. Puard, in old age, remembered clearly that the statue had long remained in his uncle's care. As a child he and his friends had baptized it Leo XIII, a detail as piquant as it is useful, since the date at which this pope attained popular fame can be exactly fixed: 1891, when he published the encyclical *Rerum novarum*. His papacy extended from 1878 to 1903. Unfortunately the exact date of Fossard's death is not known, but it was no doubt at this moment that the statue passed into the hands of Corroy, an antique-dealer at Asnière, who sold it to Dr. René Ledoux-Lebard. The doctor was a friend of Anatole France, and it was perhaps through him that the special interest of the statue came to be suspected. At any rate, Ledoux-Lebard had it photographed by Gauthier, who was then the great specialist in the photography of works of art. Large prints of Gauthier's photographs were given to the Musée des Arts Décoratifs, where they can be seen in the Maciet collection in the museum's library. Prints are also in the Institut et Musée Voltaire. Ledoux-Lebard's difficulties obliged him to entrust the statue to the Bedel repository as collateral for a loan. On the doctor's death, the debt not having been settled, his family were obliged to send the statue to the hôtel Drouot, where it was sold, in room 6, on 3 June 1953.[3] The expert failed to identify the

---

[1] According to his own statement in Georges Cain, 'La Maison de Beaumarchais', *La Cité* (Paris janvier 1905), iv. 318–19.

[2] See the drawing dated 1845 reproduced by Lenôtre, plate 10.

[3] *Gazette de l'hôtel Drouot* (Paris 12 juin 1953), p. 2.

statue, his description being as inadequate as it is inaccurate: 'Large sculpture in plaster from Houdon's studio, study for the seated Voltaire at the Comédie Française.' As the result of one of the wretched agreements between dealers that are all too common, the statue fetched the ridiculous price of 62,000 francs. After the sale it was 'knocked down' between the dealers, who had no doubt discovered in the meanwhile, or more probably before the sale, that the statue was in terra-cotta, not in plaster. Finally, after passing through the hands of two more intermediaries and having incredibly failed to interest French museums and collectors, I was fortunately able to have it acquired by the city of Geneva, at a modest price, for the Institut et Musée Voltaire.

### III

Marble is universally considered as the most noble sculptor's material. Yet it is doubtful whether this is true even when, as is seldom the case, the sculptor creates his work direct in the marble. Louis Gonse has very well said that from the point of view of the 'savour of the detail and the freedom of accent I do not know that I do not prefer the life-size terra-cotta model[1] in the Musée Fabre, and even in certain respects the original plaster in the Bibliothèque nationale'.[2] Giacometti has given definitive expression to this opinion. He says that Houdon's terra-cotta 'once modelled, is the sister of a work in marble, for its general appearance gives a faithful impression of the sculptor's work, above all by the traces of the toothed plane, the scraper and the riffler, the marks of which recall those of the graver biting the marble, and the vigorous transitions which result, serving to produce the happiest effects sought for by the masters of the sculptor's art'.[3] And again:

---

[1] Gonse uses this word imprecisely: the Montpellier mixed 'terra-cotta' and the Délices statue are replicas of the plaster original rather than copies; and of course the plaster itself is, strictly speaking, a replica of the material moulded by the sculptor's hands.

[2] Gonse, op. cit. ii. 266.                    [3] Giacometti, op. cit. i. 129.

This work of retouching, of re-handling, of accentuation was even more applied by the artist to the terra-cottas produced by moulding, so that they are sometimes mistaken for originals, even though they are in a sense only proofs.... It should be noted that Houdon often retouched them even after baking, when all further change would seem impossible. He then manipulated the terra-cotta with chisel, riffler and graver to soften or accentuate certain details.[1]

Our terra-cotta was produced by a mould, itself deriving from the original plaster in the Bibliothèque nationale, and it bears in nearly all its parts the traces of the work so graphically described by Giacometti. However, what makes this statue unique from a technical point of view is the fact that it was run into a single mould, and is not an assemblage of smaller parts. This is a rare phenomenon for a terra-cotta of these dimensions, and one that presented Houdon with a technical problem which he resolved with the practical skill which, like all great artists, he joined to his creative genius. When a terra-cotta is taken from its mould, that is, before being baked, it is relatively soft. It can be seen at the first glance that the vertical axis of the seated Voltaire traverses the chair, so that nearly the whole weight falls on its seat and legs. This presents no difficulty in marble or in plaster reinforced with iron and wood. But for a terra-cotta the problem was serious. Houdon found two solutions. The first and highly unsatisfactory one is that adopted in the Montpellier statue, in which the figure of Voltaire is in terra-cotta, but the chair in reinforced plaster. Of course this was an evasion of the problem rather than a solution. A more aesthetic and workmanlike solution was found in the Délices statue, which consists of a single 'bloc' of terra-cotta, but in which the hollow space under the chair has been filled by a pile of books.[2] This detail is consequently found only in this terra-cotta of the seated Voltaire, the only one known.

[1] Ibid. i. 132–3.
[2] M. Louis Réau thought that this might also have been intended as an allusion to Beaumarchais's great edition of Voltaire's works (private communication); 1781 seems early for such an allusion.

This is the technical description of the seated Voltaire by Houdon in the Institut et Musée Voltaire: cream-coloured terra-cotta, 'terre de Lorraine', formerly painted bronze-colour and subsequently plaster-washed; the latter has been everywhere removed, but traces of the bronze have been allowed to remain on the back; extreme dimensions: height 125·5 cm.; width 75·5 cm.; length 99·5 cm.; signed HOUDON. FÉCIT, 1781.[1]

Any literary description of this famous statue would be otiose: generations have admired it at the Comédie Française and the Bibliothèque nationale. And this is just as well, for Voltaire's own pen would be required to convey the effect of this monument of spiritualized realism. It is more directly instructive to compare the head of the statue with the terracotta bust happily also at the Institut et Musée Voltaire: this collation is an aesthetic education in itself. The two heads are clearly the same, and yet what a different impression they produce! and by what subtle means has the artist brought about this difference: minor variants in the treatment of the hair, the angle of the head, the direction of the eyes, the lines of the forehead, the fold of the lips, the curve of the eyebrows, almost invisible nuances in the modelling of the muscles!

[1] Voltaire sat to Houdon in 1778, and the sculptor executed the first models of his seated statue in 1779; he tells us so himself in his chronological list of his work, in which appears the entry: 'Two small figures of Voltaire seated in an armchair, draped in antique style, in terra-cotta and in marble and in bronze'; see Paul Vitry, ed. 'Une Liste d'œuvres de J.-A. Houdon rédigée par l'artiste lui-même vers 1784', *Archives de l'art français* (Paris 1907), N.S. i. 202; the bronze reproductions were made only in small dimensions.

# Voltaire: with a glance at Johnson and Franklin[1]

### to Frederick B. Adams

### I

IF Voltaire and Franklin have been chosen to stand at either side of Dr. Johnson on the occasion of this anniversary, the reason, I imagine, is that these two men symbolize France and America in almost exactly the same way as Johnson ideally represents England. None of these three is a typical representative of his people—to think otherwise would be to do each nation far too much honour—yet each symbolizes it in a deeper sense. Johnson is what most Englishmen think they see when they look in their mirrors: a man who is aggressively honest, sincere, bluff, conservative, religious, a hard worker when necessary, with an eye for a pretty woman but faithful to his wife, fond of animals, suspicious of foreigners. Franklin, to put it in another way, really was what every American would like to be in spirit if not in fact: a poor boy who made good, who devoted himself to the public service when he had made his pile, ingenious, inventive, sensible, tolerant, popular with men, and successful with women. Of course, these eminent figures were more than that; but the myth-making process is like a glacier: it slowly smooths away awkward features. The average Englishman would not claim to be as learned as Johnson, or the average American to be as wise as Franklin.

As for Voltaire... but let us first take a quick look at the relations between our three heroes. When Voltaire was in

[1] This lecture was delivered, 19 October 1959, on the occasion of the Johnson bicentenary celebrations at the Pierpont Morgan Library.

England, Johnson, fifteen years his junior, was a boy; when
Johnson was in France, half a century later, he made a blunder
on his own majestic scale: instead of calling on Voltaire he
visited one of the meanest of his critics, the journalist Fréron.[1]
We know what was felt by Goldsmith, Gibbon, Wilkes, Allan
Ramsay, Adam Smith, Dr. Burney, Martin Sherlock, the
glorious Boswell himself, to say nothing of Benjamin Franklin
and a hundred others (I mention here only English names),[2] on
coming into the great man's presence: but the Johnsonian
thunder and the Voltairian lightning that a meeting between
these massive natural phenomena would undoubtedly have
engendered, that, alas, we must do without. A pity! for Johnson made only two considered references to Voltaire. I say
two, for we will draw a veil over the silly gossip he decanted
in the *Life of Pope*, in which Voltaire is alleged to have talked
so grossly at the poet's table that old Mrs. Pope was driven
from the room. Chesterfield (whose manners were pronounced
by Johnson, with dubious justice, to be 'exquisitely elegant')
was far more likely to have done such a thing than Voltaire,
who was certainly not an exquisite, but who had exquisitely
punctilious standards of social behaviour.

We have two major references then. One is on a point of
Shakespearian criticism: Johnson concludes the discussion by
classing Voltaire's objections among the 'petty cavils of petty
minds' (*Works*, v. 109). This remark need not perhaps be
regarded as transgressing against the higher amenities of
scholarly debate. Voltaire replied a little, but only a little, more
courteously.[3] Incidentally, I think myself that on the actual

[1] But justice will be done! Fréron's name was omitted from the index of
Hill–Powell's Boswell's *Life*; Johnson's meeting with him is recorded at ii.
393, 406; see also the *Diaries, Papers, and Annals*, edd. E. L. McAdam and
Donald and Mary Hyde (New Haven &c. 1958), pp. 234–5.

[2] See Sir Gavin de Beer, 'Voltaire's British visitors', *Studies on Voltaire
and the Eighteenth Century* (Genève 1957), iv. 7–136; supplements (1959),
x. 425–38; (1961), xviii. 237–62.

[3] Boswell records the fact (*Life*, i. 499) but could not give the reference
because, he complains, Voltaire's works had no index; many of the fifty
collective editions of his writings published since then contain very detailed

point at issue Johnson was right, and Voltaire wrong. For in matters of aesthetic judgement the great man was sometimes just as conservative as Johnson, and less sound: in the theatre he was shackled by the dramatic laws of the *grand siècle*, and so he found it revolting that Shakespeare should have represented a drunken king on the stage;[1] his very strong feelings in this matter may now appear difficult to understand, but I dare say that many present today were thoroughly shocked the first time they saw an actress enact the part of a drunken woman. And in the eighteenth century a king was a sacred object, while in the twentieth a woman is after all not yet exactly that, even in the United States. These are matters of taste, and of morality if you like, and at least we have now learned (or have we?) that morality and taste are less absolute even than time and space.

The other reference was made when Johnson found a mistake in one of Voltaire's historical writings; on this quite minor blunder he pontificated: 'It is the great failing of a strong imagination to catch greedily at wonders. He [Voltaire] was misinformed, and was, perhaps, unwilling to learn, by a second inquiry, a truth less splendid and amusing' (*Works*, vi. 455). These words were really written by Johnson, not about himself, but about Voltaire! They cannot but provoke risibility. 'Hold, sir,' I feel inclined to exclaim to his ghost, 'Hold, sir, to accuse Voltaire of catching greedily at wonders, and of preferring the amusing to the true, is to carry prejudice beyond the limits of permissible eccentricity. This is both false and foolish.'[2]

indexes, but (note the coincidence) none found Johnson's name worthy of record in this connexion; the passage occurs in the *Dictionnaire philosophique*, s.v. 'Art dramatique' (Moland edition, xvii. 397–8).

[1] Cp. as late as 1818 the man who exclaimed 'with agony in his face, and a shrink in his frame, "Mais, Monsieur Haydon, souvenez-vous Hamlet? Ah! — de mettre une tête de mort entre les mains délicates d'un jeune Prince! Quel horreur!" '; *The Diary of Benjamin Robert Haydon*, ed. W. B. Pope (Cambridge, Mass. 1960), ii. 208–9.

[2] Goethe said that the 'first and last thing required of genius is the love of truth'.

Yet it is clear that Johnson had a proper regard for Voltaire's genius. This is obvious from his numerous passing references to him. Did he not once class him among the 'most celebrated men that have ever lived' (*Life*, iii. 263)? But Voltaire was an infidel, and that was enough to damn him in Johnson's eyes. 'All infidel writers', he once said, 'drop into oblivion, when personal connexions and the floridness[1] of novelty are gone; though now and then a foolish fellow, who thinks he can be witty upon them, may bring them again into notice' (*Life*, iv. 288). The foolish fellow who stands before you, though he lacks the wisdom to be witty, yet is so bold as to find this pronouncement hazardous. Johnson certainly regarded Voltaire as an infidel, and would have tarred Franklin with the same brush if he had given him any thought: yet who would be so bold as to claim that either man has dropped into oblivion?

And what did Voltaire think of Johnson? Well, the most rabid Johnsonian, and I gladly pin this label on myself, must admit that this question does not have too much meaning. Johnson belongs only to the English and their brethren (that is one of the disadvantages of being a sound churchman), Voltaire to all mankind (that is one of the advantages of being an infidel). In fact Johnson was little more than a name to Voltaire. He knew *Rasselas* because it was translated into French by his friend Octavie Belot; when she sent it to him he courteously found it to be 'd'une philosophie aimable et très bien écrit' (Best. 8174); the first half of this judgement seems to show that he had not read the book.[2] Boswell tells us, on the other hand, that Voltaire called Johnson 'a superstitious dog' (*Life*, i. 435)—a phrase so conspicuously Johnsonian that a measure of scepticism is indicated. However, let us assume that Voltaire really said it, and cry quits.

[1] I commend this use of the word to the attention of lexicographers.

[2] See James L. Clifford, 'Some remarks on *Candide* and *Rasselas*', *Bicentenary Essays on Rasselas* (Cairo 1959), pp. 7–14. In comparing the two stories Hazlitt is severe to Johnson, but, I think, just; see the sixth of his *Lectures on the English Poets* (*The Complete Works of William Hazlitt*, ed. P. P. Howe [London &c. 1930], v. 114).

As for Benjamin Franklin, I cannot find that he ever met[1] Johnson during all the years he spent in England; indeed, the great Cham barely acknowledged the American's existence. Again, a pity! If Arthur Lee was obnoxious to Johnson because he was 'not only a *patriot*, but an *American*' (Boswell's italics; *Life*, iii. 68), what would he have said and done if he had encountered Franklin? The thought is too strong for my imagination.

Very different were the relations of Franklin and Voltaire. When the former was in England Voltaire sent him a cordial greeting (26 February 1767), and he of course knew all about the American's scientific work. When Franklin went to France he could hardly go to see Voltaire, who lived far from the capital; for the envoy was engaged on a delicate mission, and so long a journey to visit the man the king disliked above all others would have been a gross diplomatic blunder. However, when Voltaire finally returned to Paris at the end of his life Franklin could and did call on him, taking his grandson, for whom he asked Voltaire's blessing, which the old man gave with the words, in English, 'God and liberty'. I imagine that few nowadays find this incident anything but noble and moving; it was not so at the time, for Voltaire was hated as much as he was loved, and a widely read journalist found Franklin's request indecent, puerile, base, and impious.[2]

The two men met again more than once, and most particularly at a public meeting of the Académie des Sciences. John Adams—as might have been expected—gives in his diary[3] a somewhat ill-natured account of this incident, but confirming the facts reported by Condorcet. 'The public', Voltaire's distinguished biographer tells us (Moland edition, i. 276),

---

[1] Although Professor Quinlan has shown that they were once present together at a committee meeting; see *New Light on Dr. Johnson*, ed. Frederick W. Hilles (New Haven 1959), pp. 110–11.

[2] *Mémoires secrets*, 22 février 1778.

[3] *The Adams Papers*, ed. L. H. Butterfield (Cambridge, Mass. 1961), i. iv. 80–81. Adams once called Voltaire 'as dirty a pin' as Alexander, Caesar, Cromwell, and Napoleon (letter to William S. Shaw, 16 June 1821).

'contemplated with emotion these two men seated side by side, men born in different worlds, both worthy of respect for their age, their glory, and their lives, each rejoicing in the influence he had exerted on his country. They embraced amidst universal applause, and the cry arose that it was Solon embracing Sophocles. But the Frenchman was a Sophocles who had destroyed error, and brought about the reign of reason; and the Solon of Philadelphia had based the constitution of his nation on the indestructible foundation of human rights.' This symbolic embrace of the old world and the new took place on 29 April 1778.

## II

A month later, on Sunday, 31 May 1778, a coach drove away before midnight from the town house of the Marquis de Villette, at the corner of the rue de Beaune and what was then the quai Malaquais.[1] If the torch of some link-boy or the lantern of a watchman on his rounds, for it was a dark, moonless night, had for a moment thrown a wavering light into this coach, great indeed would have been the surprise of the beholder, for he would have seen features known to the civilized world by a thousand portraits, and most recently moulded by the immortal hand of Houdon, the features of the man who is said to have been king of France when Louis XV occupied the throne, the features of the most celebrated, the most honoured, and the most hated man in Europe, the features of François Marie Arouet de Voltaire. The passer-by would have gone on his way wondering why this grand old man of eighty-four was stealing away so quietly, even secretly. He was obviously leaving Paris, that was evident from the coach and six, but why like this, in darkness and silence, behind the backs of the innumerable friends and applauding crowds by whom he had been surrounded since his return to Paris not many weeks before? Our imaginary idler might well wonder. Had he known the truth his surprise would have given way to horror:

[1] It is now the quai Voltaire.

for the features he had glimpsed were those of a dead man. Voltaire in fact had died exactly twenty-four hours before, and his embalmed body, decked in the famous dressing-gown and night-cap, accompanied by a servant whose duty it was to make the corpse simulate life, was being smuggled out of Paris.

How did so extraordinary, so uniquely melodramatic a situation come about?

### III

We have already seen that Voltaire died in Paris; he was born there, went to school there, and although he said very many unkind things about it, Paris was always for him the centre of the universe. Yet he spent hardly any of his adult life in the capital, for he was nearly always on the run or in exile: let this paradox be the keynote of our survey.

Voltaire was born when the reign of Louis XIV was at its height, and lived to witness several years of rule by the *roi soleil*'s great-grandson's grandson. He who saw the birth of a new nation, and blessed the grandson of one of its chief architects, was born in the seventeenth century. This great personal span of significant history (1694–1778) was enlarged by his early fame and by the encouragement he gave in old age to the creators of the new world. Thus it is that Voltaire is mentioned in the will of Ninon de Lenclos, born in 1615, while one of his correspondents, by no means the youngest, Du Pont de Nemours, died in 1817. Such a bridge thrown across two full centuries is more than a symbol, for Voltaire's friendship with much older men and women enabled him to know intimately the reign that began more than half a century before his birth; and he in turn nourished and inspired the men of the future.

The lawyer Arouet, though a Jansenist (the Roman Catholic equivalent of a Calvinist), sent François Marie to the Jesuit college of Louis-le-grand, perhaps because it was the best, and certainly because it was the most fashionable, school in

Paris. He thus absorbed the great Latin culture, to which he was always faithful, and the less ancient but infinitely more powerful Christian tradition, which he rejected. But he did not reject those who had taught him, and remained on terms of friendship and even affection with many of the Fathers who had been his masters. Voltaire was a brilliant student, and, it is said, an insubordinate one, but that is perhaps a little convenient hindsight. The brilliance, however, is there for all to see, expressed in his writings and in the reactions of the most intellectually stimulating group then existing in Paris, the free-thinking circle of the Temple, free-thinkers many of whom were in Holy Orders.

The members of this group joined high living to high thinking, but there again Voltaire took what suited him and rejected the rest. (It is true that he always suffered from a weak stomach.) However, his riotous sense of fun was too much for his father, who sent him off to the French embassy at The Hague, where he got into a scrape with the daughter of an adventuress, who promptly published his love-letters. He was locked up, escaped, sent home, there threatened with exile to the West Indies, and finally articled to a lawyer. It was all to no purpose, for Arouet was quite unable to cope with this extraordinary being who perhaps was not even his son (Voltaire believed himself to be illegitimate), and who never for a moment intended to be anything other than he was: and in 1718 the young man of twenty-four burst on the world with his tragedy *Œdipe*, which met with a success hitherto unparalleled, a success that Voltaire continued to enjoy as a dramatist for the rest of his life. Indeed, from now on until the end of the century Voltaire shared the honours of the Comédie Française on terms of equality, to put it no higher, with Racine and Corneille.[1]

*Œdipe* made Voltaire the head and forefront of French

---

[1] New evidence for this fact has just come to light in an unpublished Columbia thesis by Madeleine Paule Fields, *Voltaire et le Mercure de France*, pp. 95–96: during the first half-century of his career as a writer of tragedies Voltaire is mentioned in that capacity 250 times in the *Mercure de France*, Racine 210 times, Corneille 127 times.

literature, and this he remained for sixty years. The world was at his feet, the great ones of the earth were his friends, or so he thought. But to keep the friendship of kings required in those days a skill on the tight-rope that Voltaire disdained to acquire. So biting and, what was worse, so witty were his epigrams that from now on everything amusing and malicious heard at court or in the cafés was attributed to him, and presently he was sent to the Bastille for a mordant satire on the Regent which, as it happened, he had not written. Voltaire was not particularly uncomfortable in the Bastille, and indeed managed to write a first draft of the *Henriade* in his cell; but throughout his life he suffered acutely from the most potent cause of human unhappiness: a keen sense of justice. He felt his imprisonment bitterly. He realized suddenly the extent to which he was at the mercy of whimsical and all-powerful authority. First his father had threatened him with exile and a *lettre de cachet*, both sanctions which he had unquestioned power to apply to his son; and now his good friend the Regent had flung him into jail for something he had not done, after perfunctory police questioning, and without a trial. The whole of Voltaire's future life was directed by his reflections during these months in the Bastille. He realized that in future he would have to depend on himself, and that in order to be free to write as he wished, he would above all have to be mobile, and in order to be mobile he would have to be rich. This is the true inwardness of the avarice with which he has so often and so unjustly been charged—no more generous man than Voltaire ever lived.

Before he was through he had been let down or crudely betrayed by many of his friends, and by most of those he had helped, he had been again imprisoned, continuously threatened with arrest, exiled, condemned fifty times over, placed on the Index, burned symbolically by the public hangman in a dozen countries. But he had succeeded in his main objective: freedom, which he had managed to obtain only by becoming a very wealthy man. His gold enabled him to travel freely, to own strategically situated houses, always or nearly always to keep one jump ahead of arbitrary authority, in short to be free to do as he wished: and what he wished to do was to promote reason and tolerance, a Promethean task attempted with such conviction, lucidity, and unsurpassed literary genius that by middle age he had become the most influential writer in the world, which means that he was the most idolized and the most hated.

On being released from the Bastille Voltaire continued to produce plays and poems, made the round of the great country houses, got into trouble again because he tried to defend himself against a young popinjay who had insulted him, but who happened to bear the name of Rohan, was again imprisoned, and went to England. He left France a thoughtful poet, he returned a philosopher drunk with liberty. He took up the serious study of philosophy and science, fell in love with the amorous and learned Emilie Du Châtelet, retired almost completely to Cirey when the *Lettres philosophiques*, the book on Newton, and the philosophic poems got him into hot water. He had been frequently invited to Berlin, but had resisted the king's blandishments for Emilie's sake. However, when in 1749 she died in lamentable circumstances, Voltaire at last yielded, and settled down in Potsdam as the mentor of a philosopher king. Alas, Frederick turned out to be very much of a king and very little of a philosopher. The make-believe soon wore thin, and when the real philosopher wanted to leave, the real king had him arrested. When this adventure in idealism petered out Voltaire found himself homeless and alone, for Mme Denis was a burden rather than a consolation. He wandered towards the republic of Geneva, bought the Délices, thought that he had found peace, liberty, and happiness, but did not reckon with the Calvinist spirit, soon bought other houses, and finally settled at Ferney, just inside the French frontier.

From the time of his arrival at the Délices in 1755 Voltaire poured out a vast stream of books and pamphlets, plays and poems, stories and dialogues, memoranda and dispatches, histories and commentaries, in endless profusion, ranging from two-line epigrams to the *Dictionnaire philosophique* in over

2000 pages; he was translated into many languages, and his works ran into hundreds of editions; he saved the lives of many who had been unjustly condemned, and rehabilitated the memory of others already legally murdered; he enjoyed the friendship of many of the most interesting and most important people of the day (his 20,000 surviving letters are addressed to 1200 correspondents); he appeared to be fortune's darling, and in a sense he was, for he had the greatest of all satisfactions, that of seeing his ideas widely accepted by those whose opinions he valued.

But... but... but..., as Voltaire said when he was writing home what a good time he was having at Potsdam, but... he could not return to Paris. Over and over again he thought that he was on the point of bringing it off, but each time it was made clear to him that the attitude of the king and the Church would make such a visit suicidal; and it was not until 1778, in his eighty-fourth year, after nearly thirty years of exile, that the grand old man ventured to creep back as contraband to the place of his birth and the capital of his country. He was given a reception that can only be described as an apotheosis. Alone among his people, the king held back, and refused to give countenance to the presence of his greatest subject. He had already given secret instructions for the measures to be taken on Voltaire's death, and abominable measures they were: as soon as Voltaire was dead *or dying* his houses were to be minutely searched, and all his papers confiscated.[1] Allowances must be made for the young Louis XVI: he was merely too ignorant and stupid to realize that Voltaire could have been his best friend and staunchest defender: for in politics at least he had always been essentially an aristocratic liberal, as far removed from a revolutionary as can well be imagined. If such a thing as a Whig party could conceivably have existed in France, Voltaire would have been its natural leader, and there would never have been a French Revolution.

---

[1] These orders were later disowned, and were not carried out, but the documents containing them have survived.

As for the Church, well, Voltaire had attacked it for two generations with all the force at the command of a powerful genius endowed with a pen unique in its sincerity, passion, and wit. The Church, indeed, has never recovered from Voltaire's buffets, and never can, for not even the loudest polemics can drown the still small voice of a truth once spoken. Naturally, the Church defended itself, and none so foolish as to blame it. To defend itself was a duty, but was it a duty to use such very unchristian weapons, to publish monstrous allegations about Voltaire's death, and to pursue a vendetta beyond the grave? The Church's intention was to refuse burial to Voltaire's body. Yet the government knew that the consequences of such a measure would be infinitely grave, indeed it might well have led to revolution then and there. So we are treated to the interesting spectacle of ministers conspiring with Voltaire's family to defeat the intentions of their master and of the Church. Everything was prepared, the old man's last gasps were counted and measured, his death was kept a secret, and his body was smuggled out of Paris in the melodramatic manner we have seen: as contraband Voltaire had returned home, and as contraband his corpse went again into exile.

As the coach moved off it passed the spot, at the foot of the Pont Royal, where forty-eight years earlier the body of the noble, talented, and beautiful Adrienne Lecouvreur had been thrown into a ditch by order of the Church, thus evoking one of Voltaire's earliest and grandest outbursts against fanatical intolerance:

> Que direz-vous, race future,
> Lorsque vous apprendrez la flétrissante injure
> Qu'à ces arts désolés font des prêtres cruels?
> Un objet digne des autels
> Est privé de la sépulture!
> Et dans un champ profane on jette à l'aventure
> De ce corps si chéri les restes immortels!...
> Ah! verrai-je toujours ma faible nation,
> Incertaine en ses vœux, flétrir ce qu'elle admire;

> Nos mœurs avec nos lois toujours se contredire;
> Et le Français volage endormi sous l'empire
> De la superstition ?[1]

## IV

In the middle of the eighteenth century few were those in France who rose out of their poverty and ignorance. Above the people there reigned side by side religion and the law; and as Victor Hugo has said, with a passion that in no way deforms the truth, religion was intolerance, and justice was injustice. Then came the intellectual movement directed and incarnated by Voltaire. The erudite C. Constantin has expressed it admirably in the official *Dictionnaire de théologie catholique*: 'It was under the pressure chiefly of Voltaire that the modern world, in preparation since the beginning of the century, came into being, a society which, freed from the church and purely secular, guarantees to each citizen the freedom of the individual, of thought, of speech, of the press, of conscience, and of worship.' It will at once be objected that all these liberties have since been often and seriously infringed. This is only too true, and yet it is undeniable that a fundamental change occurred in human society. What then was this transformation we owe to Voltaire ? I believe that it can be expressed most precisely thus: up to a certain moment in history intellectual freedom occasionally existed by the indulgence of those in power; since that moment, when it does not exist the authorities are considered to have abused their powers. Thus defined, it will be seen that the importance of the change can hardly be exaggerated.

This transformation opened the way to man's dignity and maturity. It was the result of a slow development through many generations: the thinkers, the scholars, the artists contributed to it, each in his fashion. It would be most injudicious to attribute it to any one man. And yet.... Thus it is that the

---

[1] This poem was, of course, prosecuted, and Voltaire had to modify it; the above passage is quoted as it stands in the original edition.

image of the physical universe, as we see it, is the result of long centuries of reflection and research; but to crystallize this long process there finally arrived the right man at the right moment—and Einstein stepped on the stage. This instant, in the fierce effort of man to become really man, for man merely *sapiens* to become *homo philosophicus*, this instant, then, in the history of humanity, is called Voltaire. And just as we can fix the historic date on which our conception of the physical universe was transformed, though the philosophic moment extends through the centuries, so the historian may perhaps fix the catalytic moment of the social transformation of humanity: the moment at which Voltaire welcomed the young Calas at the Délices.

What was then the essence of this formidable phenomenon named Voltaire? He was the most typical, the most complete of all Frenchmen, the man who expressed in his own person all that was noble and subtle in the civilization whose great periods rank among the supreme moments of the human spirit—all the more so because they created the atmosphere that enabled Voltaire to manifest himself. But this Frenchman was at the same time the most universal genius of his century. He was universal because of his long visits to England, to the Low Countries, to Germany, to Switzerland; because of his numerous friendships in nearly all European countries and beyond, friendships with men and women ranging from popes, emperors, and kings to the humblest watchmakers and silk-weavers he established on his estate; because of the visits he received from hundreds of foreigners come to do him homage; because of his innumerable correspondence, which includes letters in English, Italian, Latin, Spanish, German; because of his wide and deep reading; but above all in himself, because he felt for all men, and spoke a language all understood.

We have noted briefly the paradoxes of his prodigious life—it seems impossible to speak of it without multiplying superlatives. Only an equally rapid glance is possible at the essential part of Voltaire: his work, noting in passing his style, this miraculous style all compact of grace, flexibility, energy, easy simplicity, this Voltairean style that appears to be an almost palpable extension of the writer's personality instead of a painfully forged tool, and which provides us with the most striking proof that Bernard Shaw, himself an incomparable stylist, was right when he said that 'he who has nothing to assert has no style and can have none: he who has something to assert will go as far in power of style as its momentousness and his conviction will carry him'.[1]

It is true that not even all the elegance, all the charm, and the delightful tone of Voltaire's minor poems, all the eloquence of the epistles, odes, and tales in verse, sufficed to awaken French lyric poetry from the dismal silence of two centuries. And even though Voltaire's contemporaries were convinced of the contrary, the noble epic of the *Henriade* and the agreeable *Pucelle* are very far from having endowed French literature with an *Odyssey*, an *Aeneid*, a *Divina Commedia*, or a *Paradise Lost*.

What Voltaire produced in each of these kinds would make the reputation of any other writer; but with him it is right to be severe, and easy, for what wealth remains! We have the extraordinary series of prose tales, among which *Candide* is only one, and perhaps not even the best. We have the *Essai sur les mœurs*, the first modern universal history, an eagle's flight. Its magnificent eloquence constitutes a veritable anthology of the humanist spirit and of high pros—eand deserves to be presented to the modern reader. We have the *Siècle de Louis XIV*, in which Voltaire painted the first picture of a civilization and an epoch as expressed in its ideas and its creative action. We have the *Lettres philosophiques* and the *Eléments de la philosophie de Newton* whose brilliant light expelled (for ever? let us hope so) the last shadows filled with medieval fears. We have all the iconoclastic essays sparkling with humour and erudition, hidden under alphabetic titles. We have the vast series of short and long writings even more deeply buried by

[1] *Man and Superman*, Epistle dedicatory.

the editors under the forbidding heading of miscellanea. We
have many more products of this inexhaustible fertility, but
who today has so much as heard of the *Colimaçons du révérend
père L'Escarbotier*, the *Sermon du papa Nicolas Charisteski
prononcé dans l'église de Sainte-Toleranski*, the *Mandement du
révérendissime père en dieu Alexis*, the *Instruction du gardien des
capucins de Raguse*, the *Catéchisme de l'honnête homme*, the
*Avis important d'un gentilhomme à toute la noblesse du royaume*,
and so many other wise teachings and cries of indignation?
Astonishing fact, among all these alphabetic and miscellaneous
essays there is not one that is banal or boring; all, on the contrary, even the biblical commentaries, bear on every page the
luminous evidence of what is understood by the Voltairean
spirit.

How can this spirit be conveyed in brief? When Goethe
undertook to do it he could think of no better way than to
thread a chaplet of adjectives. Let me in my turn ring the
Voltairian changes: intelligence, penetration, imagination,
comprehension, clairvoyance, wisdom, humour, courage,
generosity, compassion, tolerance, energy, verve, variety,
irony, malice, grace, finesse, brilliance, subtilty, eloquence,
knowledge, sensibility, nobility, charm, vivacity, fecundity,
style, lucidity, yes, above all and always, reason, light, truth,
and clarity.

Let us take only two passages, chosen almost at random, and
written at an interval of half a century. Here are a few lines,
in my translation, alas, from the 1727 essay *A M\*\*\**:

It was the middle of spring when I disembarked near London;
the sky was cloudless, as on the finest days in the south of France;
the air was refreshed by a soft west wind, which increased the
serenity of nature, and disposed our feelings to enjoyment: so
greatly are we machines and so much do our souls depend on the
behaviour of our bodies! I stopped near Greenwich, on the banks
of the Thames. This beautiful river, which never floods, and the
banks of which are green all the year round, was covered for a
distance of six miles with two rows of merchant vessels; all had

raised their sails to do honour to the king and queen, who were sailing on the river in a golden bark, preceded by boats filled with musicians, and followed by a thousand little rowing-boats; each had two oarsmen, all dressed as were our pages in former times, with slashed hose and small doublets ornamented with a large plate of silver on each shoulder. Not one of these seamen but showed by his looks, his dress, and his build that he was free and lived prosperously.

What miraculous simplicity! and how much colour, subtlety, and humour is covered by this simplicity that disguises art!

Let us take now the preamble to a little manifesto of 1770, the *Requête à tous les magistrats du royaume*:

The most useful part of mankind, that which nourishes you, cries to its protectors from the depth of its poverty:

You know the oppression that so often tears out of our hands the bread we prepare for our very oppressors. The rapacity of the officials in charge of our miseries is not unknown to you. You have been tempted more than once to lighten the load that bears us down, and you hear nothing from us but blessings, though choked by our sobs and tears.

We pay our taxes without a murmur, tolls, super-tolls, poll-taxes, double twentieths, obligations to the military, rights of all kinds, taxes on all that serves for our wretched clothes; and finally we pay to our priests, who in no way participate in our efforts, tithes on all that the earth accords to our labours. Thus at the end of the year all the fruit of our efforts is lost to us. If we have a moment of leisure we are dragged to forced labour two or three leagues from our homes, with our wives, our children, our beasts of labour, all equally exhausted and sometimes dying pell-mell of weariness on the way. If only we were compelled to this hard labour at moments of leisure! But it is often done just when the earth needs to be cultivated. Our harvests are made to perish in order to improve the roads....

Our fields, our vineyards, our meadows are taken from us: we are compelled to change them into roads intended for pleasure; we are torn from our ploughs to work at our own ruin, and the sole reward for this labour is to see rolling across our inheritance the coaches of the provincial extortioner, the bishop, the priest, the financier, the great lord, whose horses trample the soil which formerly served to grow our food.

All these details of our accumulated calamities do not today form the subject of our complaints. So long as we have strength we shall work; we must do so, or die.

What we ask for today is permission to work so that we may live, and enable you to live.

v

In one of the reflections, one of the fragments of himself that Pascal offered up to us, the sombre poet exclaimed: 'No longer make our lack of clarity a reproach, since it is an article of our faith. Rather let the truth of religion be acknowledged because of its very obscurity, because of the little knowledge we have of it, and because of the little care we take to know it.' To which the young Voltaire replied: 'What strange signs of truth Pascal adduces! What other signs does untruth display? So in order to be believed, it is enough to say, I am obscure, I am unintelligible!' (*Lettres philosophiques*, XXV. xviii).

When Voltaire wrote these words nearly all his life of thought was still before him, but they already contain the whole programme of this half-century of reflection and action, of creative and regenerative fecundity. They contain nearly all the key-words of the Voltairian philosophy. Our great man was in fact for light, and against obscurity; for truth, and against falsehood; for lucidity, and against unintelligibility. Voltaire unpityingly attacked the notion, unfortunately now become somewhat fashionable again, that obscurity is synonymous with profundity, and simplicity with superficiality. In truth, in order to be clear it is first necessary to have understood. 'Nothing better reveals a just and upright mind', said Voltaire, 'than the ability to express itself clearly. Language is confused only when the ideas it expresses are confused' (Best. 3550).

Thus Voltaire is opposed to revelation, to judgement by the heart, to the explanation of the unknown by the unknown.

But the reason needs facts as points of departure; vast categories of facts remain unknown to us, hence inaccessible to reason; here Voltaire does not deny, for to deny without any possibility of intellectual analysis is as little rational as to believe in the same circumstances. Therefore in metaphysics Voltaire is an agnostic, but he bows to the conventions of his time and he calls this ultimate unknown 'god' ('Deo erexit Voltaire'). One can judge the reserves made by Voltaire in this field by his highly scientific definition of the soul: 'A vague and indeterminate word that denotes an unknown principle with unknown effects.'[1]

Nor is Voltaire a moralist in the philosophic sense of the word: for him there is no innate moral sense, morality is relative, only justice and social ethics exist, born of reason.

It is thus evident that Voltaire did not believe in religion: he was also opposed to all religions, and above all to Roman Catholicism. For Voltaire religion, not being based on reason, is nothing but superstition; in a civilized nation law must be just and supreme, and religion in consequence useless. It is therefore baneful to maintain an authoritarian, dogmatic, and intolerant organization created to sustain a superstition become dangerous: *tantum religio potuit suadere malorum*.[2] Voltaire has consecrated this conclusion in the lucid, lapidary, and, at the time, triumphant exhortation, *Ecrasez l'infâme* ('Crush the infamous'). This is the phrase that Edna St. Vincent Millay had in mind:

> It is the fashion now to wave aside
> As tedious, obvious, vacuous, trivial, trite,
> All things which do not tickle, tease, excite
> To some subversion, or in verbiage hide
> Intent, or mock, or with hot sauce provide
> A dish to prick the thickened appetite;
> Straightforwardness is wrong, evasion right;
> It is correct, *de rigueur*, to deride.

[1] These are the first words of the article 'âme' in the *Dictionnaire philosophique*.　　[2] Lucretius, *De rerum natura*, i. 101.

What fumy wits these modern wags expose,
For all their versatility: Voltaire,
Who wore to bed a night-cap, and would close,
In fear of drafts, all windows, could declare
In antique stuffiness, a phrase that blows
Still through men's smoky minds, and clears the air.

Such was the negative, destructive aspect of Voltaire's
philosophy: in order to build the ground must first be cleared.
And Voltaire was able to do this because he possessed to a
supreme degree the rare and terrible faculty of doubt, the
faculty so ironically described by the historian of the penguins.[1]
And 'all great truths', as Bernard Shaw said in *Annajanska*,
'begin as blasphemies': such were Voltaire's blasphemies. It
was thus that he proved the system that appeared to his contemporaries to be an iron cage, to be in reality only a spider's
web. The destructive side of Voltaire's teaching was thus
necessary, even indispensable; but in the long run it is, of
course, the positive aspect of his ideas that is important.

What then should according to him be a society based on
reason and utilitarian ethics? First of all it must guarantee
freedom of thought. That is obvious, since truth is attained by
reflection, and is therefore endangered the moment the free
play of mind is limited for any reason whatever. Here again
Voltaire has bequeathed to us a phrase that summarizes and
perpetuates a whole philosophy: 'Freedom is the health of
the soul.'

The fundamental principle of freedom of thought deter-
mines a whole series of other freedoms. Or rather, liberty is a
chain: destroy one link and it falls apart. To reason is a discipline valuable for the individual, but thought becomes useful
to society only when it is communicated. Hence follows the
need for freedom of expression in all its forms.

However, of what use is it to possess freedom of thought
and the freedom to express one's thoughts if the latter, and
even the former, expose one to sanctions? That would be a

[1] Anatole France, *L'Ile des pingouins*, VI. ii.

Barmecide feast. Voltaire was therefore led to underline the importance of the freedom of the individual and of property, thus facing the whole problem of legal and penal reform. Nevertheless the individual is only part of the collectivity, and this collectivity is governed. This must be done in such a way as to conform to the established rules of conduct. Man needs freedom; freedom depends on law; the best government is that whose laws guarantee to every individual without distinction the maximum amount of liberty that he can enjoy without harming the other members of the collectivity.

Therefore Voltaire's philosophy can be thus summarized: man's behaviour should be based on reason, completed by social ethics and aesthetic sensibility. 'Wisdom excelleth folly as far as light excelleth darkness.'

## VI

We now observe a curious thing, so curious, so astonishing, that it was unique. I have now surveyed this prodigious being called Voltaire: very rapidly, it is true, but still I have touched on his life and his personality, his writings and his ideas. And when one has discussed the life, the works, and the thoughts of a man of letters, what is left? Nevertheless, I have mentioned only in passing that for which Voltaire is best known, which has the most contributed as much to his fame as to the effectiveness of the intellectual revolution led by him: I refer to his public activity. Voltaire was in fact the first in an honourable succession of thinkers who have thrown themselves into the fray for the good of the generality. He was also the first for twenty centuries who practised what he preached. Thus it was that he always supported the young and the talented (the list is long), and always came to the help of those overtaken by injustice (the list is even longer). Thus it was that he always stimulated around him the development of agriculture and manufactures, that he built and sowed. And all this he did not only without encouragement, but in the face of opposition

fanatical to a degree today hardly imaginable. We have seen
that power resided in the Church and the magistrature. And
Calas, to mention only one case among those with which
Voltaire concerned himself, was imprisoned, condemned, and
tortured to death by the Church and the magistrature hand in
hand. Voltaire, alone, rose up against them, his cry of indignation echoed around the world, and finally triumphed. Mankind
suddenly became aware of the fact that not even the most
crushing power can resist indignation provoked by injustice.
This lesson was taught by Voltaire. For the first time and for
good since the day on which Voltaire opened his arms to the
Calas family in the house in which I am writing these lines,
social injustice has been on the defensive: and it will remain
on the defensive so long as men retain Voltaire's gift of
indignation.

## VII

I have quoted Pascal, whom Voltaire admired as a genius of
eloquence but who represented for him the enemy: party
prejudice, dogmatism, intolerance, pessimism, obscurantism.
Here is Pascal again:

Considering the blindness and wretchedness of man, and the
astonishing contradictions displayed by his nature; beholding the
entire universe dumb, and man without light, abandoned to himself,
and as if lost in his little corner of the universe, without knowing
who has put him there, for what purpose he is there, what he will
become when he dies, I am fearful as a man would be who has been
taken in his sleep to a deserted and frightful island, and who has
awakened without any possibility of escape; and then I wonder that
we are not in despair about so wretched a condition.

The organ note is magnificent, but it is false. Voltaire has
given his reply in the *Lettres philosophiques* (xxv. vi); it is
annihilating; but I prefer to quote another reply he made in
passing, a reply that sums up all his ideas (*A une dame ou soi-
disant telle*):

I read the heart of man and often blush for it.
I examine with care the shapeless writings,
The scattered monuments and the vigorous style
Of the famous Pascal, that satirical believer.
I see that rare spirit too ready to catch fire.
    I oppose his extreme harshness.
He teaches men to hate themselves,
I should prefer to teach them to love.


Je lis au cœur de l'homme et souvent j'en rougis.
J'examine avec soin les informes écrits,
Les monuments épars et le style énergique
De ce fameux Pascal, ce dévot satirique,
Je vois ce rare esprit trop prompt à s'enflammer.
    Je combats ses rigueurs extrêmes:
Il enseigne aux humains à se haïr eux-mêmes,
Je voudrais malgré lui leur apprendre à s'aimer.

# The Love of Manuscripts[1]

*to Donald and Mary Hyde*

IT is a curious thing, and one that a psychologist or even a psychoanalyst ought to look into, that so many collectors feel the need to justify themselves. Is there anything in the least reprehensible about an occupation so innocent as assembling the little bits of paper that are used to frank postal communications? Yet who has ever met a man who admits to being a stamp-collector? No, it is a grave philatelist you see before you, who discourses about geography, the aesthetics of the miniature, and the comparative merits of engraving and offset. The man who pays ten times its real value for a pamphlet because it has a misprint on page 23 and not on page 28 will never say that he does it for pleasure, out of love of curiosities: he will talk to you very seriously about original editions and the transmission of texts, and so on and so forth—considerations which, if I, as a bibliographer, may venture to say so, are relevant about once every hundred times they are alleged. Even in what is perhaps the collector's finest sphere, works of art, an art-lover seldom buys a picture or a sculpture because he likes it: it must be by the hand of a master, or an artist who should be considered one, or who might become one. If from time to time anyone buys a picture just for pleasure he never dares admit it: it is because it recalls so clearly the old school of Murano; and of course it is of great historical interest; and of course one never knows .... For the moment I can't think of the scientific or other serious motives that inspire the collectors of match-boxes and cigarette-cards. Forgive me, I have no doubt that they exist.

[1] Address delivered at Basle, 28 June 1956, at the inaugural ceremony of the Socété suisse d'amateurs d'autographes.

Perhaps the collector of autographs is the only one who never needs to justify himself. Every autograph is a unique piece, a special source, an authentic text; and from the sentimental angle, every autograph has of necessity been actually touched by the hand that is the object of affection. There is no piece of writing totally devoid of interest. It is quite possible, indeed it happens every day, that a laundry bill yields us more important information than one of Napoleon's letters. As Pushkin said, 'We examine an autograph with curiosity even if it's only a page from an account book'. This universality, one might almost call it purity, is the outstanding characteristic of autograph collecting.

The real conserving art is not printing but writing, because the first depends on the second. No progress is possible without communication. There can be no lasting communication without writing. (Let us forget gramophone records, magnetic tape, film—new media the survival of which is still uncertain. I speak not of the media themselves, but of their products.) And we must remember that what is printed is only a very small part of what is written, and not always the most important part. The preservation of what is written is therefore a task on which may depend the future of civilization. It is a crushing task. Think, for example, of administrators' insatiable appetite for paper, which unfortunately leads to a colossal regurgitation. The accumulation of national archives everywhere has long presented a serious problem. In the United States, for example, they no longer count the acquisitions by items, or by bundles, or by collections, but by cubic feet. Thus, in the five-yearly inventory of documents produced in a little office that is part of a humble section belonging to a comparatively unimportant division of one of the government departments, one comes across a reference to 'various papers: thirty cubic feet'.

All the more reason why the lover of manuscripts should, by his intelligence, catholicity, and foresight, help to preserve those pieces which might otherwise be lost for ever.

Why do we speak of autographs rather than of manuscripts?

It is just a question of fashion, in this case a regrettable one. Of course the words are not synonymous. Not every manuscript is an autograph, though every autograph is necessarily a manu-script. The two things are equally ancient and honourable, and so are the two words. But nowadays they are not equally apt. Originally the word autograph was employed in its proper, adjectival sense—for instance, an autograph manuscript, an autograph letter. While every manuscript is written by hand, an autograph manuscript (or simply an autograph) is written in the author's own hand. But this logical sense of the words has lost a good deal of its force. Open any so-called autograph catalogue and you will find some manuscripts in the author's hand, some partly in his hand, some simply signed by him, and usually even a certain number entirely in the hand of an amanuensis. Clearly in such a state of affairs the distinction between autograph and manuscript is faint, not to say invisible.

At one time, towards the beginning of the nineteenth century, the word autograph was used only for manuscript letters. Now the notion of an autograph has gone far beyond that; there is no autograph catalogue that does not include plays, documents, literary compositions, wills, bills. In fact it is clear that nowadays the word manuscript, in its most general sense of a written (or typed!) composition, is used only by authors, publishers, and printers. Collectors, antiquarian book-sellers, autograph dealers usually use the word manuscript only for ancient or medieval manuscripts.

I wish the noun autograph would cease to be used, and be replaced by more precise words like manuscript, letter, and so on. Then we should see no more autograph catalogues listing manuscripts that for the most part are not autographs; we should have catalogues of manuscripts, of letters and documents, of illuminated manuscripts, of oriental manuscripts, and so forth, which would at least have the merit of corresponding more closely to reality.

But not so fast. My analysis has only been a superficial one. Everyone knows what a manuscript is, or thinks he does. But

as we shall see it is not as obvious as all that. Certainly, a
manuscript is a means of recording ideas, almost always with
the intention of communicating them. But that doesn't get us
very far. Everyone knows that our distant forebears were perfectly capable of communicating their ideas across considerable
distances. Let us leave aside the methods that were so to speak
immaterial, either visual, like fire, or aural, like drums. There
is nothing there for the literary amateur. We might salute in
passing the Red Indians' wampum, a belt made out of pearls
and shells, in which the shapes and colours represented quite
complicated ideas, and even whole treatises; the *quipus* of the
Peruvians, a similar system, which made use of knotted strings
(and which recalls the description of Darius's crossing of the
Ister, Herodotus iv. 98); the message-sticks of the Australian
aborigines, with notches that were partly mnemonic, partly
directly informative; and how are the colours and signs on
neolithic flints to be explained unless one allows that they have
a meaning? All these things, though not yet writing, were a
kind of graphic communication.

Writing, really writing, is not just a matter of transmitting
ideas, but of being able to transmit the words that represent
the ideas. In other words, of being able to symbolize the sym-
bols. In fact, a word is the symbol of an idea, and so the repre-
sentation of the word involves a double symbolization. This
develops in stages: first the pictograph, which represents a
whole word or even a phrase; then the hieroglyph, of which
the Chinese and the Egyptian are the best-known examples;
and finally the alphabet, which enables us to break down the
word into its primary elements, or almost.

Thus writing represents not ideas but language. But we are
still not at the end of our modest research: for is all writing
really *written*? Are the cuneiform characters of the Sumerians
and the Babylonians, and the demotic and hieroglyphic 'scriptures' of the Egyptians, really written? Sometimes they are
produced in the furnace, or carved, or engraved, or painted.
And what about the ancient metal plates, engraved or inlaid;

the tablets of clay; the *ostraka*; the wax tablets engraved by the stylus; the graffiti on certain walls, modern as well as ancient, which have been collected and published? It is clearly much easier to collect manuscripts than to define them. But I humbly propose this formula: a manuscript is a movable object with cursive writing on it. The word 'cursive' excludes everything that is not written rapidly with pen, pencil, or brush. As for 'movable', that is necessary in order to rule out, for example, monumental inscriptions, which are often painted. 'Object' is not very elegant, but what other word is there to designate all the materials used: lime-bark (the French word for book, *livre*, comes from the Latin *liber*, meaning 'bark'), papyrus (from which the word 'paper' comes), palm-leaves, linen, leather, parchment, vellum, paper?

With the word paper we are almost at the heart of the matter. It is true that most general collections of manuscripts boast of possessing some vellum, even if it is only a lease or a receipt. Really aristocratic collections include even some fragment or other of papyrus. But in general what the amateur of autographs is really interested in is paper, for long centuries the almost universal medium for manuscripts. Paper, naturally, like everything else, was invented by the Chinese. I know nothing whatever about this subject, so will discreetly refrain from any comment. Leaving aside, therefore, the manuscripts of the Far East, the most ancient known manuscript on paper is, I think, an Arabic commentary of the ninth century on the rare and curious words used by Mohammed and his followers. This manuscript is at Leyden. There are tenth-century paper manuscripts in the British Museum, in the Bibliothèque nationale, the Bodleian, the Vatican, and probably elsewhere.

The paper on which these manuscripts were written was made from cotton, and it was from cotton and other vegetable textiles that all paper was made until the nineteenth century. This industry was introduced into Europe, or more accurately into Spain, by the Moors in the twelfth century, and it is at the same period that one finds the first reference to the use of linen and hemp in the manufacture of paper. Pierre, abbot of Cluny, mentions manuscripts written on materials made 'ex rasuris veterum pannorum'. By the fifteenth century the triumph of paper was complete. By then it had replaced vellum for all writings other than legal and diplomatic ones. In our time vellum hardly survives, except for rare diplomas and other ceremonial documents. (I am speaking only of manuscripts.) The higher typography still occasionally makes use of vellum, though of course what is called vellum in the colophons of many so-called *éditions de luxe* is only very rarely real animal vellum. (In fact, printing on real vellum presents enormous technical difficulties. I permit myself this little aside because I have had personal experience in this field.)

The total victory of paper was not won without loss. To produce enough textile material for all the paper consumed nowadays would mean upsetting the economic balance of the whole world, and even so, in spite of the use of scrap, the price of paper would be very high. So other materials, primary or synthetic, have had to be found, such as wood and cellulose, to form the basis of nearly all the papers manufactured nowadays. But even the most careful manufacturing processes have not succeeded in producing from these materials a paper with real resistance, while all the papers of the middle of the nineteenth century yellow and decompose with disconcerting rapidity.

Another regrettable consequence of the mass-production of paper is the disappearance of watermarks, one of the most interesting and charming features of old paper. In some countries nowadays, including Switzerland, it is only with great difficulty that one can get paper made with a watermark. Usually the so-called watermarks that are produced are false, applied after the paper has been made by an absurd process comparable to that by which cheap wood is painted to resemble oak or mahogany.

I could go on for a long time about the history of autographs, in the proper sense of the term. But the main lines of their development are simple. If we go back to the infancy of writing, it is clear that all writing, then, is autograph. But soon writing becomes the apanage of a small minority of professionals. I leave aside the fragments of the tablets of the law preserved in various monasteries, for wicked men might question their authenticity. What is certain is that at the beginning of history, when we read for example that Jezebel wrote letters in Ahab's name (1 Kings xxi. 8), it still was not she who actually traced the words; it was probably a scribe who wrote the letters, which she sealed in the name of the king of Samaria, to lend them his authority. In the same way, when we are told that Darius signed a decree (Daniel vi. 9), the king would not have signed in the modern sense of the word, but simply have applied his seal. To find documents really written or signed by their authors we have to come down to the Ptolemaic and Roman eras of Egypt. They are mostly in Greek. In the third century B.C. they were already frequent, and include letters, many of which recall in every line how little human nature changes through the centuries. Here is one of the sad moments of life: 'Serpamonthes to Parmonthes, my brother, greeting. I have sent you the body of Senyris, our mother, embalmed, with a label at the neck, by Thales, son of Ierax, in a boat that belongs to him. The carriage is all paid. I send also the funeral notice: muslin with a pink border. Her name is written on her belly. I hope, brother, that you are well. The year 3, the second of the reign of Thoth.'

The favourable climate of the Near East has preserved these documents, while those of Greece and Rome have all disappeared apart from fragments of scrolls and tablets found at Herculaneum and Pompeii. Thus the oldest Cicero manuscript is a fifth-century palimpsest; for Virgil we have only the Schedae Berolinenses which perhaps go back to the fourth century; for Horace and Lucretius several manuscripts of the ninth century; and so on. But it is certain that the great classical writers composed their works in their own hand. There is abundant proof of this. Cicero even excuses himself, in one of his letters to Atticus, for being so busy that he is obliged on this occasion to dictate his letter to an amanuensis. Above all, the philologists and grammarians give us interesting confirmation. Thus Quintilian (*Institutio oratoria*, I. vii), discussing certain problems of spelling, appeals to the autograph manuscripts of Virgil, Cicero, the elder Cato, and Augustus. From one of Martial's epigrams (VII. xi) we learn that Rome already had a great respect, perhaps not a disinterested one, for poets' autographs: 'Pudens, you insist that I should correct my poems with my own hand and pen. Ah, you love and esteem my work too much if you want to possess these trifles in autograph (qui vis archetypas habere nugas).'

The complete disappearance of all Roman autographs makes it less surprising that not one word of the ancient Christian scriptures survives. Not a word, for example, of those epistles that Saint Paul wrote in his own hand, an unusual procedure evidently, since he emphasizes it: 'The salutation of me Paul with mine own hand', 'Ye see with how large letters I have written to you with mine own hand', 'The salutation by the hand of me Paul', 'The salutation of Paul with mine own hand, which is the token in every epistle'.

It is to the law that we owe some autographs of the beginning of our own era, because contracts had to have the signatures of the interested parties. The Merovingian kings 'signed' their decrees and treaties, and had them countersigned by their chancellors and other officials. These kings really signed in their own hand when they could write, which was not always the case. When they could not write they traced their monogram, and it was the monogram that won the day, perhaps through laziness. Anyhow Charlemagne and his successors affixed their *signum manuale*, that is, their monogram. It was only in the fourteenth century that signatures came back into fashion, and from then on the *signum manuale* was no longer used except by illiterates and the papal chancellery.

By a strange fatality we possess no literary manuscript belonging to the beginning of the Middle Ages. The oldest ones to survive indifference and accident are the chronicles of

M

Orderic Vitalis, Robert d'Auxerre, and Sigebert de Gembloux of the twelfth century, and of Matthew Paris of the thirteenth. From the sixteenth century on, literary manuscripts are plentiful, and their history is the history of their age.

The paucity of ancient manuscripts is the more surprising since there were already plenty of collectors, even in Greece, apart from official and public libraries. For example, there was Apellicon, native of Teos, later citizen of Athens. Among other exploits he bought, from the family of Neleus of Skepsis, manuscripts by Aristotle and Theophrastus. They had been given by Theophrastus himself to Neleus, who had been his pupil, and his family had hidden them in a cellar (take note of this) to preserve them from the greed of the collectors of Pergamum. Apellicon had also an ancient manuscript of the *Iliad*. But, not satisfied with all this, he found a new method which has frequently been imitated. As there were no more manuscripts for sale, he simply stole some from the archives of Athens and other cities. The wise government of Athens knew how to profit from the special qualifications of this ardent collector: they sent him to Delos to plunder the treasures of the temple.

A notable Roman collector was Licinius Mucianus, who wielded supreme power for a while before Vespasian's arrival in Rome. Mucianus got together a vast mass of speeches and letters by Romans of the republican era, together with a collection of the transactions of the senate. But it is not likely that either the speeches or the letters were autographs. Another member of the same family who shared his passion was Largius Licinius, author of the *Ciceromastix*, who offered the elder Pliny the very respectable sum of 400,000 sesterces for the manuscripts of his works, the equivalent now of about £40,000.

I cannot here go into the history of more modern collections, such as that of Montaigne, who tells us (II. xviii) that he preserved the writings of his friends and predecessors. I just draw the attention of the curious to a great and little-known bibliographer for whom I have long felt a warm affection: François

Grudé de la Croix Du Maine. Scaliger was very severe about him. 'La Croix du Maine', he said, 'is mad; he has a room crammed full of letters by various people, in cupboards, in nidis.' But he adds, 'Such people are the gleaners of the learned, hoarding up everything. They are very useful; we couldn't do without such people' (*Scaligerana*, s.n. Maine). Since it would be impossible to describe the great collections of yesterday and today, or even to mention only the most famous names, I limit myself to pointing out that we owe the two most important collections that have ever been assembled to two Englishmen, Sir Thomas Phillipps and Alfred Morrison. The first set up a small press on which he printed numerous works based on his collections. He owned so many manuscripts that it took half a century to disperse them. Alfred Morrison published a magnificent catalogue in fourteen volumes of a part of his collections, but they too have been dispersed. The only reproach that can be made against these two model collectors is that they omitted to provide for the future of their treasures.

How does one set about acquiring interesting autographs nowadays? I don't recommend Apellicon's method, although it has been followed by certain collectors, even by some of the most celebrated ones, among whom Guglielmo Libri will be for ever infamous. I must warn you that nowadays it is not easy to purloin documents from our vigilant archivists and librarians. And ours is not the age of innocence. If you steal, you will probably be caught, and if that happens I doubt whether the government of Basle would send you to Berne or Geneva to make similar acquisitions on their account. They would probably send you somewhere else. If, however, you are a kleptomaniac and there's nothing you can do about it, I advise you to follow the example of the English collector, unfortunately anonymous, who having cut off and stolen certain signatures in the British Museum, sent them back fifty years later saying that he was dying and had no further use for them.

Another way of acquiring autographs, less certain than

stealing but with its own appreciable rewards, is to find them. It is still possible to make unexpected discoveries, and it is here that the collector experiences his greatest and most worthy satisfactions. Of course you mustn't hope to come home from the greengrocer's and find your lettuce wrapped up in a Beethoven sonata or a page by Goethe: such things do happen, but mainly in the imagination of journalists in the dog days. But if you have knowledge and an alert eye, and above all luck, there are still passionately exciting surprises to be had. Suppose, for example, grubbing about among dusty old papers in an attic, you had unearthed this letter, written in a fine old hand. You would surely have been amused and touched by the innocence of long ago:

Nyon, Vaud, via Geneva.
15 February

Mademoiselle,

I send you these lines to thank you for your kindness in passing on my letters to Mademoiselle Custrin, my mistress, for whom I still have a secret passion, in spite of her infidelities and her caprice. It is still my purpose to marry her: I am easy-going, and besides I think that in spite of that bad business about the banker she will still have quite a large dowry. She plays very well; my brother Antoine will be able to accompany her on the bass viol, and we shall lead a very agreeable life, together with my cousin Jacqueline. I should be very grateful, mademoiselle, if you would give my intended the enclosed billet-doux, to be going on with until I and my family can write at greater length.

We thank you for the bale of linen you were so good as to send: we are going to make sheets out of it. As ever, we commend our cousin Etienne to their serene highnesses, and to madame la grande maîtresse. They say that their highnesses' family is the most amiable possible, and that they act plays in verse to perfection. I'm sorry I cannot see them, for I love the theatre. I was enchanted by their highnesses when you let me see them on their way to dinner. How wonderful the duchess looked, what nobility and goodness! I was in ecstasies. Her children, the little princes, were no higher than my knee. They must be very grown-up now. Dear mademoiselle, how can one help loving such a family with all one's heart, and respecting them as much as one loves them? Be good enough, dear mademoiselle, to lay our service at the feet of our noble mistress, our protectress, and believe me with all my heart your humble and obedient servant

Jacques Sutamier.

What charming simplicity, is it not? Nothing of the sort! This unpublished letter, of which I offer you the first glimpse (it is now in the possession of the Pierpont Morgan Library in New York), could not be less naïve. Not one word of it means what it seems to mean. There was no such person as Jacques Sutamier, the letter was not written at Nyon, nor addressed to a young lady, and it has nothing to do with a flirt by the name of Custrin.

It is 1760, the middle of the Seven Years War. Voltaire passionately wanted this murderous and useless conflict to end. Frederick, King of Prussia, was his friend, a faithless one it is true, but his sincere admirer. So was the Duc de Choiseul, prime minister of France. So here we have Voltaire again making proposals for peace, and transmitting their replies from one to the other. It was by no means easy: in order that his letters might reach Frederick the bearers would have to cross the battlefield. But Voltaire was not the man to be so easily discouraged: the Margravine of Bayreuth, the king's sister, was also a great friend of his, and he simply sent his letters through her. But, alas, this charming lady, the only woman Frederick ever loved, fell ill and died. Nothing daunted, Voltaire turned to another friend, the gentle and pious Duchess of Saxe-Gotha. But letters may get lost or captured; so they must be written in code. And so it was that one day the duchess, and we can imagine her surprise, received a letter which addressed her as 'Mademoiselle', and was written by a lowly stranger called Jacques Sutamier. Of course Nyon stood for Les Délices; Sutamier was Voltaire; one young lady was the Duchess of Saxe-Gotha; the other, the flirt, was Frederick the Great; and Etienne was the Duc de Choiseul—that was one of his Christian names. Only 'la grande maîtresse' is here almost under her real name, which gives us the key to the mystery. In actual fact Voltaire was very fond of Mme von Buchwald, lady-in-waiting to the Duchess of Saxe-Gotha, and always called her 'la grande maîtresse des cœurs' ('the mistress of all hearts').

So, you see, one has to be careful with old papers!

Of course the simplest thing is to inherit a collection, though it is rarely that the love of autographs is transmitted from generation to generation. What are more commonly inherited are family papers. Don't scorn these, even if they include only love-letters, marriage contracts, birth certificates, leases. Preserve them piously, add your own papers, arrange them all carefully in chronological order, away from damp and dust. And thus your children will have an heirloom which will one day be of incalculable value, or perhaps is so already. It must be remembered that the great syntheses of history are based in the last analysis on the tiny details of daily life, and that these are forgotten with horrifying rapidity. If by chance you live in a rather old house, try to establish its history: you will find that you will succeed only with enormous difficulty, and even then there will be mortifying gaps. Once again, be careful with old papers.

But in the last resort, the greater part of nearly all amateur collections is acquired by a method that is simple and open to all; that is to say, by purchase. You may say that this method is as open to all as the Grand Palace Hotel. This is a common error, due to the mistaken ideas entertained by those who have not yet acquired the passion of collecting. Of course, if you want to build up what I have called an aristocratic collection, beginning with papyri, going on through the noblest of illuminated manuscripts, and finishing up with letters by Rubens, Calvin, Ariosto, Cervantes, Rabelais, and Christopher Columbus, or even with series of letters by lesser people—if your ambitions are of that order, you'll need to be rich—even very rich. But if your aims are more modest, if you are satisfied, to begin with, just to make agreeable and interesting purchases that will bring you inexhaustible pleasure—well, if such is the case, a collection of autographs is within the reach of almost everyone. I shall come back to this in a moment.

But first I should like to put you on your guard against one of the autograph-collector's great dangers—fashion. Few collectors are safe from this tendency, which is as unintelligible as it is unintelligent. A letter by a painter brings a fabulous price at auction; and immediately everyone starts to collect artists' manuscripts. A manuscript by a famous astronomer is found in a cellar, and the rush begins, everyone is after the literary remains of scientists. But I repeat, this is a dangerous way of going on. The wise beginner will not be led astray. Of course, it is not at all easy to know what is the real value of any manuscript, because the price it will fetch is the result of a subtle interplay of imponderables: the existence of a manuscript which its owner is more or less anxious to sell, and that collectors are more or less anxious to buy. At auction, these forces have free play, at least in theory. But suppose a dealer in autographs issues a catalogue, how does he arrive at his prices? I prefer not to try to penetrate these mysteries. But one thing that's certain is that the collector as well as the dealer is entitled to his views on the subject. I hope I shall not expose myself to reprisals if I whisper to collectors who are just beginning that the price asked for a given manuscript is not an absolute one, as in the case of a current postage stamp. It is a suggestion rather, which naturally the vendor can stick to if he wishes. And if it seems to you a fair price, don't argue.

What, in fact, would be the right price for a Shakespeare manuscript? Ten thousand pounds? fifty thousand? a million? It is impossible to tell, since no manuscript of his is known. What is certain is that if one day such a manuscript should come on the market, many public libraries and private collectors would fight for this precious relic, and with reason. But in this sphere there are very great oddities. It is understandable that an autograph by Petrarch or Molière should fetch a high price, because these are geniuses whose work has been admired by generations of readers all over the world, and autographs by them are rare. But is it not absurd that the mere signature of a certain Button Gwyneth should fetch an equal price? In the same way, it seems astonishing that manuscripts by Napoleon and Nelson should be so dear, although they are very numerous. This is not too logical, obviously, but it is understandable. It is simply that the demand by collectors who wish to possess their autographs is no more limited than the supply. Take the case of the manuscripts of Karl Marx. Buyers are keen but few. If prices are high it is because as things are autographs by Marx must be considered rare. In fact he wrote thousands of letters to socialist organizations all over the world. Many of these societies have vanished, it is true, but if the survivors were one day to dispose of their archives, the price of Marx manuscripts would come tumbling down. Lastly there is the case of people so famous and of such universal appeal that they are above the laws that usually operate. Here the classic case is certainly Voltaire. Autographs of his are extremely numerous, but the prices have been continually rising for two centuries, and are now increasing more rapidly than ever, unfortunately for me.

Another thing I deplore is the exaggerated prestige of unpublished manuscripts. Many collectors, in fact, are prepared to pay much more for an unpublished text than for one already known. But a distinction must be drawn. A letter or a poem that tells us something new is important. Its importance derives, though, not from the mere fact that it is unpublished but from the new information it gives us. So obviously from this point of view the manuscript of a text already published can be much more important than the manuscript of an unpublished work. The majority of published works, even quite recent ones, are reproduced very inexactly, and even, very often, with unbelievable inaccuracy. Thus, in the most recent edition of Voltaire's works, not one of his letters has been printed entirely correctly. The case of other great writers is little better. But that sentence or line or even word which someone thought it 'necessary' to leave out or alter, is often for that very reason the most revealing, and almost always more valuable than some other text which may be unpublished but of no special interest. In any case many so-called unpublished texts are nothing of the kind.

One last warning: beware of imitations! Actually, astonishingly few forgeries have been perpetrated, but there are some, and precautions have to be taken. You must either rely entirely on reputable dealers, which you can do with perfect confidence, or, what is infinitely preferable and much more interesting, you can train yourself to be an expert in your own right, and guard against imposture in that way. But the essential thing is to develop a critical sense, which gradually becomes a kind of instinct or intuition. For intelligence and knowledge alone are not always enough. Take, for example, the case of the learned Michel Chasles. He was clearly a man well above the average in intelligence and knowledge: he was a member of the Académie des Sciences and the author of a *Traité de géométrie supérieure* and a *Mémoire de géométrie pure sur les propriétés générales des cônes du second degré*. Furthermore, he certainly did not lack historical sense; on the contrary, he had published the *Trois livres de porismes d'Euclide*, a famous *Histoire de l'arithmétique*, an *Aperçu historique sur l'origine et le développement des méthodes en géométrie*, and other works of the same kind. Nor was this all. He even had quite a specialized knowledge of the field with which we are dealing, having contributed to the *Catalogue des manuscrits de la Bibliothèque de Chartres*. He was also an enthusiastic collector. In short, the ideal man.

Now one day in 1861 a certain Vrain-Lucas introduced himself as the representative of a family of émigrés who possessed a remarkable autograph collection. They would be prepared to part with certain items to such a distinguished collector as Monsieur Chasles. He leapt at the offer, and became the proud possessor of letters and other documents bearing the signatures of Rabelais, Molière, Abelard, and Raphael. Then, his appetite now thoroughly whetted, Monsieur Chasles pressed the mysterious family for the even more remarkable manuscripts that Vrain-Lucas had hinted at. And it was not long before Chasles had been offered, and had accepted, a safe-conduct in the hand of Vercingetorix, letters from Pythagoras to Aeschylus and Sappho, from Alexander to Aristotle, from Archimedes to Nero, from Lazarus to Peter the apostle, from Mary Magdalene to her brother, and from Cleopatra to Julius Caesar. I don't need to tell you that they were all false. But how had Vrain-Lucas succeeded in forging letters in such ancient and diverse languages? Quite simple. He did not go to any such trouble. Mary Magdalene and Cleopatra, Archimedes and Lazarus, all wrote in French. Even more interesting, they all had very similar handwriting. I have actually seen many of these documents, and there can be no doubt about it. And what about the intelligent and learned man of science, the historian and palaeographer, Michel Chasles? Well, Monsieur Chasles, neither mad nor in his dotage, had no doubts, bought the autographs in thousands, and defended Vrain-Lucas vehemently against sceptics. The farce would have gone on until the protagonist's death if he hadn't made a serious mistake: he began to forge modern letters, by Galileo, Newton, Pascal; and inevitably these contained mistakes that could be checked. This was going too far, and Vrain-Lucas (neither the first nor the last of the forgers, but certainly the only genius among them by virtue of his almost innocent effrontery) was prosecuted, condemned, and imprisoned. I only add that there are now sure scientific methods for discovering forgeries. May the shade of Michel Chasles protect you!

But let us return to the question of prices. Since the commercial side of autographs is after all of cardinal importance we mustn't shrink from going into details. Besides, I do not want to deprive beginners of a little solid encouragement. So let us look at the fixed-price catalogue of one of the oldest and most respected firms of autograph dealers.

What do we see? First that there are plenty of manuscripts for sale. That is something; and very important too, because it shows that one can buy worth-while items without special research or superhuman patience. We should also notice that the fixed-price catalogues of this firm are issued in two parts, one of which is devoted exclusively to autographs at moderate prices. There is no need to emphasize how important this is for the beginner. The next thing we notice is the striking diversity in the prices. The most expensive item costs the equivalent of £200. It is an astronomical manuscript of the thirteenth century. Yet this must not deceive us. This price is only a modest fraction of what we should expect to pay for a manuscript or group of papers of the first importance. But if we look at the other end of the scale we find an impressive list of interesting autographs available at the equivalent of a few shillings. For less than £1 one can own a letter from the British prime minister Lord Aberdeen; General Baker, who took Napoleon on board the *Bellerophon*; Cardinal de Bernis, statesman and poet; Boissy d'Anglas, member of the Convention; the Maréchal de Boufflers; the attractive English painter and engraver, Boys; the Baron de Breteuil; Lazare Carnot; the first Prince of Condé; Daubenton the naturalist; Dreyfus; Joseph Bonaparte; Gambetta; Guizot; Louis-Philippe, and others. As you see, neither variety nor interest is lacking. And we must remember, in justice to our charming enemies the autograph dealers, that such catalogues are not prepared and printed just for profit. One can easily imagine what proportion the costs of administration, cataloguing, and printing bear in the case of a catalogue of items priced so low.

But let us continue. Even £10 is still quite a modest sum in comparison with what one pays for other objects that bring only passing pleasure. Well, according to these same catalogues, for about £10 you can acquire an item signed by Alembert; fourteen folio pages, annotated by Kellermann, concerning the secret expenses of the army in Italy; an order dictated by the emperor to Maréchal Oudinot during the battle of Leipzig; a letter by Claude Bernard; a sheaf of letters by Camille Borghese, the husband of Pauline Bonaparte; thirty-two

letters by Maréchal Canrobert; the autograph manuscript of
a little comedy by Carmontelle; a very interesting letter by
Charles II, king of England; a letter from Chateaubriand to
Suard, and so on. So it is incorrect to think that autograph
collecting is the prerogative of the rich.

Let us move to an even higher plane. When we get to £50
or £100 we are clearly in the region of figures beyond the
means of many collectors, though they would not hesitate to
pay such a sum for something to wear, a piece of jewellery, or
a little holiday. But let us glance at the marvellous items one
can own for sums of this order: an important letter of Georges
Cadoudal, one of the leaders of the Vendée; an important diplomatic letter of Charles I, king of England; a signature on vellum by Jean Dunois, the Bastard of Orleans, Joan of Arc's
companion in arms; 58 folio pages, words and music, of
Gounod's *Marche au calvaire*; a fragment, 18 pages, of the
same composer's *Romeo and Juliet*; a whole sheaf of accounts
relating to the death of Marceau; a long and curious letter by
Stendhal; the draft of an important letter from Barras to the
citizen consul Bonaparte; a document, uncommon to say the
least of it, on which one finds the signatures of Louis XV,
Marie Leszczinska, the future Louis XVI, Louis XVIII, and
Charles X, several other members of the royal family, together
with that of the Marquis de Sade; a letter from Louis XI to
Louis d'Amboise and his other counsellors; an item signed by
La Fayette and Lasalle, bearing the seal of the Committee of
Petitions and that of the City of Paris, and many more.

I make no excuse for dwelling on the question of prices.
Anyone who is chiefly interested in this aspect of the matter
will never make a real collector; but no collector can disregard
it without neglecting his duty towards himself, his family, and
other collectors. All I wanted was to demonstrate beyond all
possible doubt that a worth-while collection of autographs is
really within the reach of all. I think I have done so.

In short, an autograph collection built up with intelligence,
care, and method will never lose its market value. On the

contrary, it will be a safe and profitable investment. For it is an undeniable fact that manuscripts, so long as one is not carried away by whim or fashion, represent some of the most stable of all values. It must also be remembered that a group of items which are comparatively unimportant taken separately may, when brought together, constitute a quite valuable whole. For example, you can, for a few shillings, buy a manuscript of almost any French eighteenth-century poet, with a few exceptions. But assemble a more or less complete range of examples of the same manuscripts, and you will have a collection that is valuable in every sense of the word.

I will now allow myself to address a few remarks to collectors of fairly ample means. Many of them build up well-organized collections, and have a definite object, which they pursue with intelligence and ardour. I salute them. They are deserving of all praise. Posterity will be grateful to them and will not forget their name. But there are many who buy only as the fancy takes them; others who pursue only very dazzling items; many others who are guided only by the latest fashion; and some who become traders rather than collectors and are ready to sacrifice any part of their collection to make a good profit. (Let me add in parenthesis that there are even some collectors, *horresco referens*, who are capable of one of the worst possible crimes in this sphere, a crime against humanity: they refuse to make their manuscripts available to scholars. Sometimes they have reasons, I wouldn't call them valid, but understandable. Unfortunately all is not pure and noble even in the world of manuscripts. We know there may be some who have bought manuscripts with money acquired on the black market, or others who use this as a way of evading income-tax. But that is no excuse for the small minority who are merely selfish and indifferent. Let us blush for them, and may the face of the Lord be against them.)

But let us return to our subject. There are certain categories of autographs that even the most far-sighted collectors neglect; I refer in particular to large archives. And here may I make a serious appeal? Everywhere, and especially in France, there are many collections of family papers preserved, if I may use so inappropriate a word, in dilapidated châteaux. These papers mean nothing to their owners, who would part with them gladly to any collector who knew how to set about it. I myself know of several archives of this kind, belonging to famous families and people, which contain inestimable treasures. How dreadful it is to see these collections of unique items going mouldy, gnawed by mice, drenched by rain seeping through cracked ceilings, neglected, unknown, while some well-known page that has been reproduced a thousand times passes from one collection to another, leaving a deposit of gold in the dealers' willing hands with every move! Why don't collectors who have the means and the room take an interest in such collections? Think of the pleasure of sorting them, cataloguing, publishing them, and—who knows?—perhaps making sensational discoveries among them!

I have tried to show you what the love of autographs is—a passion which, far from being unhealthy, is pure and beneficent. How many friendships are sealed on this honourable field of battle; what a pleasure it is to save from loss or destruction some fragment whose value one has recognized; what a happiness to be able to help a scholar in the difficulties of research! And at the end of our lives, after we have fulfilled our duty towards our families, what a tranquil pleasure and deep satisfaction, to give or bequeath our collection to some public body, so that our efforts may be consecrated by the good of posterity! *Noblesse oblige.*

# INDEX OF NAMES

*(The names enumerated on pages 117–18, 171–2 have not been indexed)*

PRINTED IN GREAT BRITAIN
AT THE UNIVERSITY PRESS, OXFORD
BY VIVIAN RIDLER
PRINTER TO THE UNIVERSITY